# Women, Church,
## *and* Leadership

# Women, Church, *and* Leadership

New Paradigms

*Essays in Honor of Jean Miller Schmidt*

EDITED BY
Eunjoo Mary Kim *and* Deborah Beth Creamer

PICKWICK *Publications* · Eugene, Oregon

WOMEN, CHURCH, AND LEADERSHIP
New Paradigms: Essays in Honor of Jean Miller Schmidt

Pickwick Publications
An Imprint of Wipf and Stock Publishers
199 W. 8th Ave., Suite 3
Eugene, OR 97401

www.wipfandstock.com

ISBN 13: 978-1-60899-901-9

*Cataloging-in-Publication data:*

Women, church, and leadership : new paradigms ; essays in honor of Jean Miller Schmidt / edited by Eunjoo Mary Kim and Deborah Beth Creamer.

xxx + 186 p. ; 23 cm.—Includes bibliographical references and index.

ISBN 13: 978-1-60899-901-9

1. Schmidt, Jean Miller. 2. Women in Christianity. 3. Women clergy. 4. Feminist theology. I. Kim, Eunjoo Mary. II. Creamer, Deborah Beth. III. Title.

BV639 W7 W456 2012

Manufactured in the USA

# Contents

# Foreword

## Roots, Risks, and Rudders:
## Leading the Church

### Mary Elizabeth Mullino Moore

THE CREATORS OF THIS volume were inspired by the witness of Jean Miller Schmidt, who was an illustrious leader in Iliff School of Theology, and also gave leadership to a new era of Methodist theological studies and to emerging movements of women in the church and theological education. She was a pioneer, but not the first woman to do what she did. She found her roots in the women who went before her—long before her—as testified in *Grace Sufficient*. She found roots in her own life with God. Her roots were so deep that they held true when she was called to stand against the actions of other leaders, or pace her writing so she could give her best to teaching, or adjust her life to family needs. Her roots were so deep that she could take risks, and she did. She apparently had invisible rudders below the surface of her life that kept her steady and guided her journey.

The purpose of this book is not to do a biography of Jean Miller Schmidt but to take cues from her life and work to guide leadership in the church today—leadership that is boldly led by women, deeply engaging of diversities in the human family, adventurous in communication, and resistant to consumerist culture. I am honored to write this foreword to support a movement of leaders—Jean herself, the thoughtful authors of this book, and women and men across the world who take risks daily and contribute to a better world.

I begin with stories, uncovering some of the risky realities of leadership and the urgent need for new forms. These are composite stories from diverse North American communities.

- A congregation began ministering with homeless people in their neighborhood, many of whom slept and ate in the church and some of whom participated regularly in worship and classes. Yet, this church received a lecture each year from a church official about needing to grow its membership numbers. The pastor was eventually moved to a new community, and the next pastor was told that his job was to grow the church.

- Another pastor was asked to begin a new church, which grew into a congregation with a strong sense of mission. The church's mission was not to serve the poor of their city, but *to be the poor* in service to others. The people began ministry after ministry, built a supportive fellowship, and established a community garden and food bank for their own families and their neighbors in need. Yet, they found little support from church structures.

- A leader in the GLBTQ community initiated a ministry with prostitutes and pimps who sought to survive on the streets. This leader felt called to walk with these people and to help them find God and new life. She credited the church for bringing her back to Jesus when her life was most hollow and self-destructive; she wanted to offer that opportunity to others. Yet, she was eventually asked to take this ministry outside of the church.

What went wrong in these stories? Were the ministry paradigms too unusual to grasp? Did the leaders and congregations cross acceptable margins? Or do institutions simply have difficulty accepting and supporting ministries on the margins—egalitarian ministries serving a wide range of the human family, as Gail Murphy-Geiss identifies with American Methodism?

This book is about leadership. What kind of leadership is needed in local communities and in denominational structures to support the kinds of risk-taking, path-breaking ministries I have just described? The measures of effectiveness may need to change. The paths of communication between church leaders and local communities, and between denominational leaders and congregations, may need to change. The passion to serve the poor and marginalized cannot simply be a word from the top that is enacted in traditional, safe ways; it has to bubble up from local communities and grow organically from those communities. This passion will finally lead to new models of church *and* new models of leadership, a topic broached in the introduction of this volume (Eunjoo Kim and Deborah Creamer) and explored throughout the book. Here is where I turn to images of *roots, risks, and rudders.*

## Roots

God is the taproot of leadership in the Christian church. As Catherine Kelsey writes, "The theological purpose of Christian communities of faith is to cooperate with the *missio Dei,* what God is doing in the world expressly through Human Spirit." There are other roots as well because ministry is enacted in the particularities of living communities. Kelsey focuses on the particular communities of the Wesleyan movement, such as the classes. Katherine Turpin focuses on the witness of GLBTQ clergy who follow an overwhelming call to remain in ordained ministry within a denomination that officially condemns and denies them. Dan Geslin, in response, focuses on the witness of GLBTQ clergy who are overwhelmingly called to *leave* their denominational home and make a home elsewhere in order to be true to themselves. Deborah Creamer and James Burns focus on the strengths of human limitations, and the realities and possibilities of living with disabilities (all manner of disabilities). These are only a few examples of the different ways in which the *missio Dei* is revealed and enacted in the lives of Christian leaders. The roots for one leader may seem strange to another. *Missio Dei* is shared, but the particular roots of an individual leader or community of faith differ according to the gifts and challenges that are particular to them.

## Risks

In my work as Dean of a theological school, I find that the community is strongest when it is rooted in a common mission, yet people function best when they draw upon their unique gifts, passions, and experiences. This sounds somewhat safe until one recognizes how much risk is involved in following one's deepest passions and drawing wisdom and strength from one's own roots. For the leaders in the three stories I shared, the passions they followed were shaped by their unique life experiences and the unique experiences of the congregations in which they served. By drawing from their own wisdom, they found themselves imbued with passion and in the midst of powerful, marginal, and unpopular ministries.

## Rudders

So how do people lead risk-filled ministries with little support from their institutions? What rudders will guide our leaders? The primary rudder is *God's Spirit* moving in human lives, emphasized by Catherine Kelsey. Eric Smith sees this rudder as an antidote to superficial efforts to be relevant; he urges leaders to attune to Spirit by cultivating "active expectancy." Another rudder is the *community* itself, which can fruitfully shape preaching, according to Eunjoo Kim, as well as other forms of ministry. Holly Heuer connects this rudder of community to Trinitarian images of mutuality, and she presents ways in which a leader can practice mutuality in shared preaching. Another rudder is *engagement with difference and difficulty*, like the gender differences and expectations that Melanie Rosa describes and the difficulties posed by those differences. Penny Rather builds on Rosa to highlight diverse traditions, practices, and measures of success, all of which, like gender, have potential to enrich the church and its ministry. Carrie Doehring intensifies these ideas, making a case that intercultural engagement contributes to spiritual deepening and stretching. Such engagement requires and nourishes trust, both in God and in other people. Elizabeth Randall adds that relating deeply to diversity is not easy; it requires time and intentionality. Finally, a rudder is found in reimagining the church as a place of *refuge* where God is ever-present and people are encouraged to gather, risk, and trust. Amy Erickson challenges the church to become new, even as her respondents (Vernon Rempel and Janet Forbes) see the new kinds of leadership that a "refuge" church will demand.

The rudders suggested in this book can support people with "extraordinary calls," as named by Jean Miller Schmidt and highlighted by Elaine Stanovsky—calls that come from God, require high commitment, and are blessed with God's grace. Such leadership is deeply challenging; it pushes leaders to question many conventional images of the church and assumed values of leadership. Yet we cannot rely on demands for accountability to renew the church; we need new models and the courage to move into them. This challenge is not for the fainthearted, but it *is* for the faithful, and God's grace is sufficient!

# Preface

## Tink Tinker (wazhazhe / Osage Nation)

THIS VOLUME HONORS THE career of Dr. Jean Miller Schmidt as teacher and churchwoman, as a theological historian, a writer of important books on Methodist history and the protestant "social Gospel" tradition, and a superb critical thinker. In a world (not least of all, a theological world) badly in need of change, Jean became the first female professor at Iliff School of Theology more than three decades ago, immediately and radically changing the way that the school conducted its business. After thirty-two years on the faculty, Jean retired as the Gerald L. Schlessman Professor Emerita of Methodist Studies, leaving an indelible imprint on the Iliff School of Theology—on students, on faculty colleagues, on staff, and on Iliff's public constituency. Students consistently found her to be a favorite professor throughout her tenure at Iliff. At the same time she became a churchwoman of renown in both Methodist and broader ecumenical circles, including work with the World Council of Churches. Her most creative gift to theological education and the well-being of the church, however, came in the form of an important curriculum innovation that transformed the way history is taught in schools of theology.

I had been on the faculty for only four years when Jean approached me with what was then an incredibly novel pedagogical idea. Like most schools today, Iliff had already made the shift away from teaching "church" history to teaching the history of Christianity, a subtle but important shift—tailor made for this University of Chicago graduate. Jean was responsible for teaching the school's course on the history of modern Christianity, the fourth of the usual sequence of history courses required in most seminaries and schools of theology for students in M.Div.

programs. Jean's vision was to treat the subject quite differently than it had been taught in any M.Div. program. The history of modern Christianity was taught largely from a vantage point that traced the triumphal spread of one or more denominations, usually emphasizing the development of post-Reformation theologies in the Euro-Western context and perhaps especially the development of churches in the United States. Others had, of course, included the spread of Christianity in a more global context, tracing the work of missionaries in one or more denominational tradition. Jean's vision was different and much more unsettling to the conventional theological development of divinity students.

I was a decidedly junior faculty person at that time, yet as Jean described her idea to some of us, she chose to include me much more intimately in the project. She wanted students to do more than just accumulate a chunk of factual knowledge about that past. Her notion was to press students to reflect deeply on the relationship between the spread of Christianity, including within their own denomination, and the spread of European colonialism. What was the complicity of the churches in establishing the social and political order of the modern world and, perforce, our contemporary world? What was the role of the churches in the colonial projects of Europe? As European countries began to use their military might to carve up the rest of the world for their own economic empowerment, what was the role of the churches in undergirding that imposition of power? These were the concerns that Jean brought to me as she envisioned a thorough renovation of her required course. Jean was clear. She wanted that radical reading of history from the underside from beginning to end. This new course would decenter the usual "northern" reading of the history of Christianity and challenge the ecclesial order of things.

"Our" course would begin with the history of Christian missions to Indian peoples alongside of the conquest of those same Indian peoples. It would move through the conquest of North America and then treat the results of missionary colonialism in Africa, Asia, and Latin America, with an emphasis on reading those histories from the perspective of the people targeted rather than from the perspective of the Euro-Western missionaries. It would not be easy, especially emotionally easy, for White American students to work through a history of Christianity from this perspective. At the same time, reading this history from the perspective of the colonized of the world would force all students to reflect more deeply in rethinking their theologies.

That a scholar from Jean's particular social location might have engaged this sort of methodology was remarkable in itself. Her own social context was that of a White, middle-class, faithful Methodist woman. Her own class interests and her status in a largely White and middle-class denomination were not intuitively well served by this pedagogical shift. Jean, however, was committed to the greater interests of truth, social change, and transformation. The project took enormous courage, yet Jean's courage was always wrapped in a quiet spirit of gentleness that always characterized her entire presence. As a teacher, as a scholar, and as a colleague, Jean was widely respected by the whole Iliff faculty, yet her courage and vision especially won the hearts of her colleagues of color. She was a consistent ally to the pedagogical and theological interests of these scholars of color in our ongoing argument for diversity in theological discourses. Her commitment to this sort of transformation was at the heart of her teaching.

This presentation of "Christianity in the Modern World" proved to be decentering and challenging to our students—who came to Iliff, after all, in order to train for service in the churches, the very churches whose history we unearthed in such a way that any romantic heroizing of any denomination was no longer possible. But Jean carried herself pedagogically with such grace and gentleness that students continued to come back to the table to learn more. Her style was provoking without ever becoming confrontational. It always seemed that Jean was able to touch students in ways that simultaneously challenged and yet affirmed them. Indeed, everywhere I travel in the country, I meet former students who always want to talk about their memories of Jean and her classroom. They want the latest news about her and her work. Jean's students serve today in churches, in social justice agencies, and in academic positions where they use their theological sense of history learned in her classroom to influence a whole new and broader generation of committed Christian folk and young scholars in many different denominations and academic institutions.

I am honored to have been Jean Miller Schmidt's close colleague, and delighted to have this opportunity to express my personal gratitude for her friendship and for the twenty years we spent together in the classroom. Her gentle yet bold and resolute spirit has greatly influenced me as a teacher and shaped my own vision for engaging theological and historical academic discourses. Calm tranquility along with forthright and dauntless courage most characterized this scholar. It made her a class act that will not soon be forgotten.

# Acknowledgments

A VOLUME LIKE THIS one only emerges through the encouragement and support of an entire community. As editors, we wish to express our deep thanks to each of the authors who shared their insights, passions, scholarship, and time with us in making contributions to this volume. As both scholars and pastors—and, each one of you a leader in your own right—your reflections here are creative, thoughtful, substantial, and demonstrate so well the breadth of possibility for women, leadership, and the church. We are so glad you partnered with us in this work.

We express our appreciation to all of our colleagues at the Iliff School of Theology for their support of this project, particularly to the dean of the faculty for financial support and to the entire faculty for their engagement with the themes and ideas addressed in this volume, through colloquia and other formal and informal settings. We also thank the Iliff Writing Lab and the numerous doctoral students there who assisted with proofreading and editorial formatting.

We want to acknowledge and give thanks to Wipf and Stock Publishers for their interest in our project. Christian Amondson and Diane Farley, your professional and timely assistance made it possible for us to share this volume in public.

Finally, we join with all of the contributors in this volume in expressing our profound appreciation to and love for Jean Miller Schmidt—colleague, teacher, scholar, mentor, and friend. Jean, you have formed each of us in ways you will probably never fully know, and we are so grateful.

# Contributors

## Foreword and Preface Authors

**Mary Elizabeth Mullino Moore**, Dean of the School of Theology and Professor of Theology and Education, Boston University School of Theology

**George E. (Tink) Tinker** (wazhazhe / Osage Nation), Clifford Baldridge Professor of American Indian Cultures and Religious Traditions, Iliff School of Theology, Denver

## Chapter Authors

**Deborah Beth Creamer**, Associate Dean for Academic Affairs and Director of Library and Information Services, Iliff School of Theology, Denver

**Carrie Doehring**, Associate Professor of Pastoral Care and Counseling, Iliff School of Theology, Denver

**Amy Erickson**, Assistant Professor of Hebrew Bible, Iliff School of Theology, Denver

**Catherine L. Kelsey**, Visiting Assistant Professor in Theology, Gerald L. Schlessman Chair in Methodist Studies, Dean of the Chapel and Spiritual Formation, Iliff School of Theology, Denver

**Gail Murphy-Geiss**, Associate Professor of Sociology, Colorado College, Colorado Springs

**Eunjoo Mary Kim**, Professor of Homiletics, Iliff School of Theology, Denver

**Melanie Rosa**, District Superintendent, Mile High/Pikes Peak District of the Rocky Mountain Conference of the United Methodist Church

**Katherine Turpin**, Associate Professor of Religious Education, Iliff School of Theology, Denver

## Respondents

**James Burns**, Pastor, Metropolitan Community Church of the Rockies, Denver

**Janet Forbes**, Senior Minister, St. Luke's United Methodist Church, Highlands Ranch

**Dan Geslin**, Pastor, Sixth Avenue United Church of Christ, Denver

**Holly Heuer**, Pastor, Calvary Presbyterian Church, Denver

**Elizabeth Randall**, Rector, St. Andrew's Episcopal Church, Denver

**Penny Rather**, Minister of the Unitarian Universalist Fellowship of Laramie, Wyoming and adjunct faculty in the Religious Studies Department of Naropa University, Boulder

**Vernon K. Rempel**, Senior Pastor, First Mennonite Church of Denver

**Eric Smith**, District Superintendent, Peaks and Plains District of the Rocky Mountain Conference of the United Methodist Church

**Elaine Stanovsky**, Bishop of the Denver Episcopal Area of the United Methodist Church

# Introduction

Eunjoo Mary Kim *and* Deborah Beth Creamer

## Church in the Twenty-First Century

IN TWENTY-FIRST-CENTURY NORTH AMERICA, the Christian church faces a decisive shift in the theory and practice of church leadership. The term *leadership* may generate a good number of attempts at definition. As some researchers have examined, it is indeed virtually impossible to define an integrated concept of leadership.[1] However, when applied to Christian communities, the word leadership certainly opens the door to scholarly and pastoral conversation concerning the cultivation and development of the vital ministry and mission of the church from biblical, theological, and pastoral perspectives. Church leadership is many-faceted and takes on new meaning in different circumstances, at different times, with different problems. It is a commitment to develop and articulate a new vision for the church and to choose different modes of action through which the vision can become a reality. Therefore, church leadership is not only compatible with faithful ministry but also essential to the fulfillment of the calling of God to which we have responded.[2]

Changes in culture inside and outside the church challenge clergy and lay leaders alike to reconfigure both their identity and their leadership roles. The internal and external elements of the challenge to church leader-

---

1. Weems, *Church Leadership*, 15. According to Harris W. Lee's research on leadership studies over the past fifty years, there are at least 350 definitions of *leadership*.

2. Weems, *Church Leadership*, 35.

ship can be explained in at least four ways. The first element is a change in gender roles within the church. In contemporary North America, mainline churches and even churches once viewed as socially conservative have seen dramatic increases in the numbers of female clergy and lay leaders. This presence has steadily eroded traditional roles that limited women's leadership of the church[3] and has challenged many churches to reconsider a model of leadership, authority, and power quite different from the traditional ecclesial structures of hierarchy. These changes mandate that the contemporary Christian church pay more attention to the development of women's leadership in particular and church leadership in general from women's theological and experiential perspectives.

The second element of the challenge to the church is related to the condition of our globalized world. Contemporary churches live in the midst of a multiracial and pluralistic culture, in which one of the crucial issues is the matter of diversity. Our twenty-first-century world connects the local and the global more closely than ever before in human history; there is no purely homogenous religious group, whatever that might mean. Christian churches are no exception. Their internal and external environments are becoming more multicultural and multiracial. The local context for ministry is no longer isolated from the pluralistic global culture of the wider world. Many congregations consist in diversity, including those who are from different races, different denominations, and different religious backgrounds, as well as different gender, sexuality, and age groups. Such a changing environment challenges church leaders to reflect on the identity of the Christian church in a constructive way and demands that they make a decision whether their churches will attempt to become "safe havens" from difference or will seek to embrace others who have historically been excluded from church leadership. Based on such

---

3. Currently about fifteen Protestant denominations allow women to be pastors. 23 percent of United Methodist Church clergy are female (http://www.gcsrw.org); in the Presbyterian Church (USA), women are about 30 percent of active (nonretired) clergy (http://www.pcusa.org/pcnews/2006/06538.htm); the Evangelical Lutheran Church in America reports that the percentage of its ordained clergy who are women doubled from 1991 to 2003 to 16 percent (http://www.elca.org); according to The 1998 Episcopal Clerical Directory, 13.8 percent of those listed were female (http://www.episcopalchurch .org); in 2000, women made up 21 percent of Disciples of Christ clergy (http://www .beliefnet.com/Faiths/2000/07/Women-Clergy-The-Numbers.aspx). See Pitts, "Women, Ministry, and Identity." In this article, Pitts indicates changing gender roles in the leadership of conservative Baptist churches as part of the evolving identity of Baptists.

decisions, their leadership styles regarding worship, preaching, teaching, counseling, and other pastoral ministries will be different.

The third element of the challenge to Christian ministry is a shift in communication modes. The twenty-first-century congregation lives in a changing culture influenced by the advancement of communication technology. It is crucial for contemporary church leaders to recognize the shift from a print culture to a screen culture and its significant impact on their congregational lives. Computers, television, cellular phones, video projection, and other media have influenced our Sunday worship and preaching styles as well as shifted our everyday pastoral communication methods. Moreover, many churches now benefit from the technology of the World Wide Web to share their ministries with unknown members of the virtual community. In this era of technological transformation, church leaders are challenged to think of how to practice new forms of communication in which visual images are the dominant language as well as how to address substantive issues beyond the geographical boundaries of the local church.

The last but perhaps most critical element of the challenge to church leadership is the negotiation of the church with the culture of consumerism. In fact, increasing secularization and the resulting congregational membership decline are the most crucial and realistic issues for many mainline American churches. As a way to restore their membership rolls, many of them adapt consumer-oriented market strategies and tactics to their church growth movements. They are tempted to see evangelism as some kind of commodity procedure, in which people are regarded as consumers and the church's role is that of "selling" the gospel wrapped by the sweet promise of worldly prosperity, at the cost of losing the gospel of the Cross. Consumerist culture often leads both clergy and laity to confuse church leadership with an effectiveness-production model of corporate leadership in capitalistic and business culture.

Encountering this crisis of cultural shift, contemporary churches need to inquire about biblical and theological understandings of church leadership under the guidance of the Spirit of God. The practice of leadership should inspire congregations to center their existence and ministries in the power of the Spirit that brings new life out of disorder and death beyond all human measure. A renewed understanding and practice of church leadership should be able to see clearly, substantially, and systematically, ways in which theology comes into human action and in which human action shaped by theological thinking contributes to the "redemptive transformation"[4] of person, churches, and cultures in a perilous age. Consequently, churches with such renewed leadership can awaken the deeper longing of the congregation for a relationship with the living God.

## Women and Church Leadership

In the face of these challenges to church leadership in North America, this volume is a scholarly and pastoral response to the urgent demand for the renewal of church leadership. The seventeen contributors to this volume strongly felt a need to research new paradigms for church leadership and thus participated in this collaborative project with their wisdom and knowledge, their experience and imagination.

The Iliff School of Theology provided the historical momentum to make their efforts come true through the publication of this volume. In December 2008, Dr. Jean Miller Schmidt, the first female faculty person in the history of Iliff, retired from her thirty-four-year professorship as Professor of Modern Church History. She was hired in 1975, was tenured in 1979, and secured the endowed chair of Gerald L. Schlessman Professor of Methodist Studies from 2001 to the time of her retirement. Not only as the first woman on the full-time faculty at Iliff but also as one of the first female church historians in her field, she represented women's voices in the world of academia and church as well as within the school. She pioneered to teach gender-related courses such as "Women and the Church" and "Women in American Religion" in 1976 and participated in numerous scholarly and ecclesial events by publishing books and articles, giving lectures, leading workshops, and chairing committees.

Among her publications, her monograph *Grace Sufficient: A History of Women in American Methodism* represents her great interest in women leaders in the United States and her fervent concern for the transformation of church leadership from the perspective of women. In this book, Schmidt reminds us of the generations who came before us, preparing the path over which contemporary female leaders have walked with gratitude, and reclaims a lost harmony muted by the male-centered leadership of the church, which is entirely insufficient in its concepts of church leadership. She has demonstrated this new model of leadership in her

---

4. Wright and Kuentzel, *Redemptive Transformation*, 12.

own life, offering a gentleness that is quite different from weakness, a keen sense of relational power, and a sense of grace that is apparent to all those around her. Her own leadership grew out of feminism as a formative process of finding voice and creating relationships, recognizing her call to be a leader even before women's leadership of this sort was acknowledged or accepted by the institutions around her. Such experiences gave her a foundation from which she could balance her love for the history of Christian churches with her attention to areas of struggle and challenge. She is known as a student-centered teacher, and as a guide and mentor who offers the gifts of careful listening and encouraging, emphasizing dialogue and one-on-one conversation even as she attends strategically to larger institutional issues. She has been central not only in creating the Iliff ethos as it exists today, but also in challenging and encouraging us to form new generations of church leaders for service to Christ and the Church with new paradigms of leadership relevant to our particular historical contexts.

When the female faculty of Iliff gathered to celebrate Professor Schmidt's retirement, we acknowledged that there was more to be done for the transformation of church leadership from women's points of view, while also affirming and celebrating the progress that had been made. We also agreed to publish an edited book based on our research on the contemporary Christian church and its leadership, hoping that this could be a significant contribution to an understanding of church leadership from the perspective of women as well as a meaningful and fruitful way to inherit and evolve Professor Schmidt's legacy.

To this volume eight female scholars from various fields of theological education were invited to contribute by researching and writing their essays about church leadership. Just as Friedrich Schleiermacher once strongly pointed out, they firmly believe that "the leadership in the church is the final purpose of theology"[5] and propose new paradigms of church leadership in relation to their specialties and particular interests. Nine pastoral leaders from seven different denominations were also invited to this collaborative project as conversational partners. They participate in discussion by sharing their pastoral responses to the essays, in which they offer their practical insights into how the essays can be understood and applied to real ministerial settings. The pastoral leaders were chosen with

5. Schleiermacher, *Christian Care*, 99.

the intention to bring diversity in gender, race, sexuality, and denomination. They serve either local churches or denominational offices in roles such as bishop or superintendent.

The essays and pastoral responses included in this volume aim to equip church leaders to be able to clearly see the sociocultural structures of contemporary churches, society, and the world, as impacted by radical shifts of gender roles, diversity, technological transformation, and the lure of consumerist culture. Moreover, each chapter helps readers reconfigure the theological and biblical foundation of church leadership in light of women's experiences and theological understandings. The authors encourage readers to develop and practice creative, responsive, and relational leadership, relevant to their particular ministerial contexts. Ultimately, this collaborative project between academia and church attempts to bring new life to ministry and ministry to new life. It provides the church with the clues for renewed leadership for the critical and decisive years ahead by challenging it to rethink its identity, renew its vocation, and revitalize its ministry with fresh insights and passion.

## New Paradigms of Leadership

The essays contained in this volume propose new paradigms for church leadership. A type or a model is normally understood as a pattern for imitation or emulation. The paradigms proposed in this book illustrate new approaches or perspectives as a conceptual point of view in relation to many crucial topics emerging from the contemporary Christian church. In developing these new paradigms, perspectives of women are consistently used as the primary tool that provides coherence and convergence for dealing with a variety of topics. These new paradigms contribute to the cultivation and renewal of leadership styles of church leaders in creative and relevant ways.

The eight chapters focus on three guiding themes: Women and Church, Women and Ministry, and Women and Scripture. Part 1, Women and Church, takes up core sociohistorical analyses of leadership in the American church and critically explores the nature and function of ecclesial leadership based on women's experiences and theological insights in order to present constructive new paradigms for the church.

Gail Murphy-Geiss's essay, "From Side Street to Main Street: American Methodism in Social Contexts," critically reviews social and ideological contexts for women's leadership in the American church. She reminds us of the richness of its history, particularly that in the early American Methodist movement, women's voices were encouraged in a counter-cultural and spiritually egalitarian atmosphere. Murphy-Geiss points out that women played crucial roles in the establishment, expansion, and nurturing of early Methodist societies, while later, as the Methodist movement institutionalized into an official denomination, the freedoms women once enjoyed became more limited and confined by an increasingly conventional and firmly established hierarchy. Her analysis of those changing contexts provides contemporary church leaders with practical implications for developing their leadership based on understanding their particular sociological and historical contexts for ministry.

In her response, Bishop Elaine Stanovsky pays special attention to Murphy-Geiss's warning that the institutionalized United Methodist Church may constrain the work of the Holy Spirit to control the system of the church. Stanovsky convinces us that the Holy Spirit is working today both inside and outside the structure of the church with new "extraordinary calls" to a new generation of disciples and offers church leaders some practical ideas to revitalize the church, based on women's ministry in early Methodism.

Deborah Creamer describes in her essay, "Inclusive Ecclesiology: A New Model of Hospitality," the ways in which ecclesiology, as the study of the Church, is a profoundly theological undertaking as well as a sociological, historical, and practical one. To demonstrate this, she explores issues of disability, particularly the ways in which individuals with disabilities have experienced barriers to hospitality in communities and congregations, sometimes due to physical and architectural barriers but more significantly due to attitudes and even theological understandings about disability. Creamer sees hospitality not as a false welcoming of "the other" but as the affirmation of the presence of diversity, breaking down false dichotomies and admitting the distinctiveness and fundamental value of each of us within God's creation. As part of this shift, she demonstrates how our models of God inform our understandings of each other, and explores ways in which new models of God might invite even broader possibilities for inclusion. She suggests that attention to disability as an issue of genuine hospitality allows us to consider ways to become more accessible to all those who presently experience a lack of welcome. In these ways, Creamer helps readers stretch their theological perspectives with a vision for a genuinely inclusive ecclesiology.

James Burns responds to Creamer with affirmation that her theological concept of God based on "the limits model" is appropriate to interpret our reality. Burns shares his personal experience of ministry and illustrates the relevance of Creamer's theological approach to preaching and other areas of ministry.

Catherine L. Kelsey's essay, "Holy Spirit, Communities of Faith, and Leadership," attends to the particularity of human relationships, a common emphasis among women in leadership, and builds on the theologies of Wesley and Schleiermacher with her own observation of leadership in faith communities. She proposes that the theological purpose of Christian communities of faith is "to cooperate with the *missio Dei*, what God is doing in the world expressly through Holy Spirit." Focus on this purpose allows her to observe two specific practices of effective leaders, practices that make it possible for them to be effective and for the communities they lead to participate in the mission of God.

Eric Smith, in his response, agrees with Kelsey that the church ministry should be "a God movement" inspired and touched by the Holy Spirit, rather than "a human program." He suggests the practice of *lectio divina* as a way to cultivate "a Holy Spirit–rich environment" in which church leaders can listen to both the divine Spirit of God and persons diverse in their communities.

In part 2, Women and Ministry, four chapters focus on the four fundamental areas of pastoral leadership—preaching, vocation and identity, spirituality, and pastoral care and counseling. Each chapter proposes a new paradigm of leadership from women's perspectives and provides insights into the practice of new leadership models.

In her essay, "Preaching as an Art of Shared Ministry," Eunjoo M. Kim analyzes the contemporary context for preaching and reviews the history of preaching from the woman's perspective. She considers pastoral leadership the most challenging issue for female pastors, as well as for male clergy, who realize that traditional patriarchal leadership is now dysfunctional, and proposes that shared leadership be a new paradigm for the preaching ministry. Kim defines shared leadership in a new way and reconfigures preaching not as a tactic or strategy but as an art through which the congregation experiences holistic transformation personally and collectively. She also offers a practical theological methodology for the practice of preaching as an art of shared ministry.

Holly Heuer further explores theological challenges in Kim's essay and shares a variety of her personal experiences of preaching as a shared ministry in her particular congregational setting. Based on her experience, Heuer values shared preaching as a theological practice of ongoing dialogue on the gospel within a congregation.

Katherine Turpin's essay, "Drag and Other Practices of Unauthorized Leadership," explores Judith Butler's concept of drag as a strategy for social change practiced by GLBT persons ordained in denominations who will not recognize them openly. Turpin argues that while staying in denominations without full acceptance is often equated with political inactivity and being "closeted," such a practice may potentially contribute to an exposure of the exclusionary assumptions inherent in ordination standards, may increase the social legitimacy of GLBT clergy, and may create in the minds of congregants a necessary shift in the notion of what is possible. By making comparisons to the history of women's ordination in the Methodist tradition, she suggests that the practice of performing clergy identity prior to its legitimation by the broader body may contribute to the eventual transformation of exclusionary structures and policies within these denominations.

In his response, Dan Geslin reflects on his personal experience as a GLBT person who had to leave the denomination of his childhood because of his sexual orientation. Based on this experience, he reminds readers how hard it is for GLBT pastors to practice the "drag" strategy in their ministerial settings. He also points out serious ethical issues emerging from the practice of ministry "in drag."

Melanie Rosa explores in her essay, "Leading with Grace: Authentic Leadership in the Church," the spiritual leadership of women—past, present, and future. According to her research, religious women have consistently practiced a courageous style of spiritual leadership in spite of the numerous limitations imposed upon them historically in a fundamentally masculine institution. She examines the spiritual leadership of particular women throughout history, offers examples of women leading in the church today through relational evangelism and the empowerment of others, and proposes "authentic leadership" as a new paradigm for the future.

Penny Rather, a Buddhist practitioner and Unitarian Universalist parish minister, relates Rosa's concept of authentic leadership to her denominational situation and ministerial experience. In her response, Rather reminds us of the Buddhist teaching of the eight worldly *dharmas* (phenomena), which is insight into emptiness, and introduces a variety of spiritual practices of meditation as ways to nurture the inner life of leaders and an experimental mindset, which is the core of authentic leadership that Rosa proposed.

Carrie Doehring explains in her essay, "Women's Experiences and Intercultural Spiritual Care," that the practice of intercultural spiritual care is a way to deeply engage religious and cultural traditions within a spiritually, socially complex world. She critically evaluates the leadership of feminist theologians and practitioners in the field of pastoral care at the end of the twentieth century, including womanist approaches. Doehring affirms that their focus on women's experiences of pastoral care, both as care givers and care receivers initially privileged the uniqueness of women's embodied experiences and contributed to breaking paradigms of care articulated by male pastoral theologians and practitioners. However, she states, shortly after the emergence of feminist and womanist approaches to pastoral care in the 1980s and 1990s, female leaders in the field of the practice of care realized that a woman-centered approach was not enough and that more radical intercultural approaches were needed to do justice to the complex diversity of spirituality and suffering as experienced by persons, families, communities, and social systems. Drawing a parallel between Schmidt's examination of the particularities of Methodist women's experience of grace-sufficient and women's embodied experiences of grace-sufficient in a diverse cultural world, Doehring insists that an intercultural approach to spiritual care challenge contemporary pastoral leaders to take seriously the radical kind of trust that is needed to practice pastoral care.

In her response, Elizabeth Randall examines her personal journey as a pastor. She reflects on her pastoral ministry in the past and the present and is convinced that Doehring's "metaphor of the trifocal lens" is greatly helpful for her to improve her ministry in the future. By listening to and seeing others through the "trifocal lens," Randall states, her ministry in pastoral care and preaching will be more inclusive and sensitive to diversity within her congregation.

Part 3, Women and Scripture, challenges us to think biblically about the image and role of the church. Rather than simply revisiting the gender issue within Scripture, Amy Erickson's essay, "Zion as Refuge: A Metaphor with Implications for the Church in the Postmodern World," offers fresh insights into reconfiguring the identity and function of the church from the biblical point of view. More precisely, Erickson explores the various layers of the Zion-as-a-refuge metaphor in the Psalter, and illumines a new image of the church based on that image. She reminds us that cities in the ancient Near East were presented as feminine, and convinces us that the metaphor of Zion as refuge is a rich and multifaceted symbolic language that has the potential to be life-giving to women. Erickson challenges the prevailing understanding of the feminine image of Zion which is limited to the traditionally feminine realm such as nursing, birthing, nurturing, mothering, and so on, and extends the concept of the feminine image of Zion into the image of protection as a fortress. According to her, the fortress image of Zion metaphor shifts traditional feminine constraints of Zion as the subordinate wife of the deity to the image of cosmic refuge, a place that symbolizes divine power and offers continuing access to God. Erickson goes even further by emphasizing that because the city is associated with God's presence, Zion itself points to God's self. She relates this radical concept of the metaphor of Zion to the issues of Christian social ethics and stresses that the feminine image of Zion represents a place where God is present and available to God's people. This implies the identity of the church, that is, a locus of spiritual and physical renewal, as well as a sanctuary to all who are threatened by war and oppression.

Two thoughtful and practical responses are given to Erickson's essay. Janet Forbes pays special attention to the refuge image of Zion in relation to her pastoral experience with postmodern spiritual seekers. She emphasizes the significance of the ministry of refuge and suggests that pastors should be "the soul friend" to spiritual travelers and that the church should function like a "way-station" for them where they can find meaning and purpose of life and experience holistic healing. Vernon K. Rempel focuses on the transforming power of metaphor in the liturgical life of the church. He reminds us that churches today need new metaphors that can provide us with meaning in our changing lives. In addition, Rempel takes seriously the significance of the feminine image of Zion against our male-centered culture and insists on female leaders' active roles in liturgical and ecclesial space.

Academic essays and pastoral responses to chapters enhance the practical theological conversation between theological scholars and pastoral leaders by offering ways to think together about crucial issues for the church. These are profoundly theological, practically insightful, and historically timely proposals of new paradigms of leadership for the contemporary church. The new paradigms of leadership proposed in this book promise to be most helpful in renewing the leadership of the church and its vocational commitment to transform the world.

# BIBLIOGRAPHY

Pitts, Bill. "Women, Ministry, and Identity: Establishing Female Deacons at First Baptist Church, Waco, Texas." *Baptist History and Heritage* (Winter 2007) 71–84.

Schleiermacher, Friedrich. *Christian Caring: Selections from Practical Theology.* Translated by James O. Duke. Philadelphia: Fortress, 1988.

Schmidt, Jean Miller. *Grace Sufficient: A History of Women in American Methodism,* 1760–1939. Nashville: Abingdon, 1999.

Weems, Lovett H., Jr. *Church Leadership: Vision, Team, Culture, and Integrity.* Nashville: Abingdon, 1993.

Wright, Dana, and John Kuentzel, editors. *Redemptive Transformation in Practical Theology: Essays in Honor of James E. Loder, Jr.* Grand Rapids: Eerdmans, 2004.

# PART ONE

*Women and Church*

# Chapter One

## From Side Street to Main Street
### *American Methodism in Social Contexts*

### Gail Murphy-Geiss

IN HIS MOST INFLUENTIAL work, C. Wright Mills describes the best so-cial science as that which "deals with problems of biography, of history, and of their intersections within social structures."[1] He called this system of analysis "the sociological imagination," but he did not intend that it be limited to sociologists. Indeed, Mills hoped that a sociological imagina-tion would be a quality of every social scientist. As he saw it, the challenge for all such scholars is in attending to the last part of the statement—the intersections. Biography and history cannot be studied separately, for human beings are not the same across time, and historical periods are not simply sequential stories of individual lives: that is, microhistory of the individual must consider its place in the larger social context, while macrohistory must not be blind to the individuals who enact it. For Mills, a truly perceptive understanding of society requires a serious examina-tion of people's lives as embedded in the structures and institutions of their times.[2] *Grace Sufficient: A History of Women in American Methodism*

---

1. Mills, *The Sociological Imagination*, 143.
2. Ibid., 161.

1760–1939 is just that kind of history, because its author, Jean Miller Schmidt, is a historian with a sociological imagination.

One indication of a sociological imagination is the inclusion of multiple levels of analysis. That is, a rich sociohistorical analysis should consider all three levels of society over time: the individual agents (the micro), the institutional structures (the macro), and the intermediate level groups that make up much of social life (the meso). *Grace Sufficient* does this well. The individuals analyzed in the book are mostly women, many of whom were little known and continue to exist only in their diaries, letters, obituaries, and grave stones. The institutional structures explored are the large scale historical forces of the period covered, particularly industrialization, urbanization, the end of slavery, and the first wave of the feminist movement. The intermediate level is the various movements and eventually denominations that led to what is now the United Methodist Church. All three levels are recounted and integrated in a complex story covering almost 200 years, providing the reader with a full picture of extraordinary private lives in rapidly changing social contexts. Those same people in different times may have lived very differently, and many other individuals in that same period chose different paths as well. There is nothing inevitable about these stories. Still, history can only be fully understood at the intersections of particular people in specific times, and it is that same sociological imagination that can help contemporary church leaders understand the promise of our time as well. But before moving too quickly to the present, let us look more carefully at Schmidt's sociohistorical analysis in *Grace Sufficient* as an important record of the past, and as a model for understanding the intersections of agents and structures in our own day.

## The Macrolevel: Widespread Structural Contexts

Three of the major large-scale contextual factors of the time period covered by Schmidt are industrialization and urbanization, the abolition of slavery, and the first wave of the feminist movement. Understanding each of these is essential in recognizing some of the opportunities as well as the limitations that American Methodist women faced.

Attentive to industrialization and urbanization, Schmidt puts the deaconess movement into context by reminding readers that "the women who answered the call to deaconess life were part of the massive rural-urban shift in the United States in the last quarter of the nineteenth century."[3] Similarly, Schmidt attributes the decline of the deaconess movement to a number of social factors, among them the increasing employment opportunities for women in the secular realm. As women moved to the cities and discovered industrial labor and the independence that came with an income of their own, deaconess work became only one among many options available to women. In fact, from this new perspective, the deaconess option looked rather traditional compared with the many exciting new opportunities for women of that day.

New opportunities for women were not shared equally among all women though, depending especially on race, and to a lesser extent, region. The system of southern slavery was supported by a highly patriarchal culture, in which white women were valued as "soft, submissive, weak and dependent," particularly as compared to "the image of the strong, commanding, intelligent and protective southern man."[4] Schmidt notes that these white women rarely if ever challenged their "masters," for fear that the entire slave system would have been destabilized, risking the wealth and power of all whites. As a result, most southern women went to great lengths to live up to the image of the ideal southern belle, for their own benefit and that of their children. However, while outwardly submissive, both white and black women expressed their inner struggles in their diaries, as they tried to make sense of "religious yearnings . . . in a racially stratified society."[5] Given these limitations, it is not surprising that southern women's diaries were seldom written for public consumption, and therefore, rarely published. Acceptable social roles for southern women were more limited than for northern women, who were permitted to take more visible leadership roles. In other words, while industrialization and urbanization opened up new opportunities for women in the north, the slave system confined southern women, limiting their public activity. These contextual factors made certain realities more or less possible for individual women, depending on each one's situation.

The first wave of the feminist movement was another important contextual factor for all women (and men), and Methodists were no exception. Perhaps the best example of the intersection of a macrolevel historical

3. Schmidt, *Grace Sufficient*, 210.

4. Ibid., 90.

5. Ibid., 144.

context (in this case, feminism) and a microlevel biography (individual agent) meeting in a mesolevel institutional context is in the story of Frances Willard and the Women's Christian Temperance Union (WCTU). Willard was an early leader of the women's prohibitionist movement, who served as the President of the WCTU from 1879 until her death in 1898. The WCTU was formed in response to extensive alcohol abuse by men, and the initial goal was the closing of saloons. Because this was a solution dependent on structural changes, women's suffrage became a corollary issue of concern. Willard believed that women would have to be able to vote (for prohibition) in order to protect themselves and their children from the alcoholic abuses of men, a campaign she referred to as "The Ballot for Home Protection."[6] But over time, Willard began to see the home as broader than "four square walls" and that the special work of women was to "make the whole world homelike."[7] Schmidt characterizes the power of Willard's ideas this way: "Under her 'Do Everything Policy,' thousands of Victorian 'ladies' left the sanctuary of their homes and moved into active participation in a wide range of issues, including women's suffrage, social (sexual) purity, concerns of labor, peace and arbitration, welfare work, temperance education, and health."[8] Here, we see how much of the power of the early feminist movement was rooted in the efforts of traditional church ladies, articulated by and personified in the charismatic figure of Frances Willard—a talented individual addressing the larger social issues of her time through the opportunities afforded her by a budding feminist movement that was already laying the groundwork necessary for her vision of structural change.

The consequences of women's organizing in this period went well beyond the issues listed above. Women began to travel unaccompanied to meetings, to serve as administrators and leaders of local and even national organizations, and to build networks with other women and men toward the realization of their goals. Those goals were often attached to an ideology of home that was both traditional and expansive, something Schmidt and others have called a "soft feminism."[9] Some women went even further in the expansion of their sense of "home," becoming foreign missionaries. They did so both as the wives of missionary men and on

---

6. Gifford, *Writing Out My Heart*, 7.

7. Willard, *How to Win*, 112.

8. Schmidt, *Grace Sufficient*, 157–58.

9. Lindley, *You Have Stept*, 88; Schmidt, *Grace Sufficient*, 178.

their own as single women, often supported through the fund raising efforts of other women organized in church-based missionary societies. Schmidt clearly sets these efforts into social context, saying that the appeal of foreign mission work, "can only be understood by appreciating that when middle-class (white) women began to reemerge into the public sphere in the second half of the [nineteenth] century, the church provided the framework within which they could 'test their wings' and develop the necessary skills."[10]

## The Mesolevel: Methodist Opportunities and Limitations

Early Methodism in England, led primarily by John Wesley, was a countercultural reformation movement in reaction to the highly institutionalized, hierarchical, and ceremonial Church of England. The movement was marked by four radical ideological features: piety, individualism, reductionism and perfectionism, all well suited for import to the young United States, where such ideas were more readily embraced.[11] Schmidt notes that, "There was a radical spiritual egalitarianism in this early Methodism that tended to oppose the worldly hierarchies of race, gender and class."[12] That is, in Methodism, those on the margins of society could find a sense of self worth, empowerment, and even independence, all of which made the movement particularly attractive to white women, African Americans, and the poor. Women truly found their voices especially through the ideological elements of individualism and reductionism. The focus on individualism encouraged women to practice holiness and to take charge of their own pursuit of perfection. Through reductionism, or the rise of lay ministry, women not only saw to their own holiness, but encouraged it in others through teaching, exhorting, and in some cases, even preaching. Both individualism and reductionism were practiced in intense communities of mutual challenge and support, another powerful element in the Methodist formula for success. These groups provided a site of real affirmation for women and other marginalized people, many of whom lived in isolated locations across the American frontier, or were segregated in other ways from the centers of society, as for example, slaves were.

10. Schmidt, *Grace Sufficient*, 177.

11. Gaustad, *A Religious History*, 144.

12. Schmidt, *Grace Sufficient*, 51.

With growth in membership, it became impossible for the Methodist movement to retain its radical edge. The "laws of increasing group size"[13] dictate that successful sects become denominations, partly through a need for greater coordination and an increasing diversity among members. As leadership develops to coordinate the growing organization, regular members become less intensely committed, and total consensus becomes untenable among the growing diversity of opinions. In the case of Methodism, another casualty of the "success" of growth was the increasing control of women. For example, before 1803, there were at least forty-two Methodist women preachers, but in 1803, an official ruling announced that women were only to address other women.[14]

One response to growing limitations on women's roles was the Deaconess movement. Schmidt dates the true beginning of the Deaconess movement to 1887, when Lucy Rider Meyer gathered a group of women to help her in visiting and aiding poor immigrants in Chicago.[15] Then in 1888, the General Conference gave the Deaconess Movement official sanction as a recognized ministry of Methodist women and described the bulk of the work as: ministering to the poor, visiting the sick and dying, caring for orphans and the homeless, and comforting the afflicted—all of which seemed perfectly suitable work for women. Not surprisingly, the work was to be overseen by Annual Conference Boards appointed to the task, the majority of whom, by rule, could be men. At that same General Conference, women were denied seats as lay delegates, even though five had been elected by their Annual Conferences and had traveled to the Conference intending to serve.

Despite the early activities of some notable women preachers, Methodist women's battle for full clergy rights was hard fought and long. Although the Methodist Church did not grant full ordination to women until 1956,[16] many women and their supporters had sought licenses to preach and/or ordination for over a century and a half before. John Wesley himself had granted permission to a handful of exceptional women to preach during his lifetime, but that practice came to a rapid end once the official Methodist denomination was formed. Still, there were always

---

13. Johnstone, *Religion in Society*, 70.

14. Schmidt, *Grace Sufficient*, 32.

15. Ibid., 200.

16. Chaves, *Ordaining Women*, 150.

some, even if only a few, who objected to the new limitations. Some women left for other denominations, some became travelling preachers and foreign missionaries, and others accepted positions in local churches which allowed them to preach, despite denominational objections, when possible. The story is long and complicated (partly because of the multiple denominational streams which eventually became the United Methodist Church) and filled with interesting characters on all sides. It suffices to say that the fact that women wanted to preach and be ordained for hundreds of years and were successfully denied until 1956 is a testament to the effectiveness of male denominational control of women through most of the history of Methodism. On the other hand, the stories of the fighters and the success stories, even if it meant leaving the denomination, are a testament to Wesley's original precedent which honored the power of experience over unjustifiable tradition. There was a radical spiritual egalitarianism in Methodist theology that continued to confront the increasingly conservative church structures— something that could not be silenced, despite the powerful forces of institutionalization.

Grace might have been sufficient to carry these Methodist women through the many trials of their lives, but Methodism, at least in its earlier movement form, was proficient in creating an ethos which allowed for their leadership. Schmidt's sociologically imaginative history identifies not only the individual Methodist women who pushed institutional Methodism when it was limiting, but she also recognizes the mesolevel space of radical Methodism which created new opportunities for women in the first place. That push and pull between radical movement and conservative denomination are at the center of the story, somewhere between the structures of the larger society and the individuals who spent their lives in pursuit of both personal and social holiness.

## The Microlevel: Extraordinary Cases

John Wesley and Mary Bosanquet each used the word "extraordinary" in their letters to one another regarding the feasibility of women preaching. Bosanquet wrote to him that although she did not expect all women to be called to preach, she believed some to have an "extraordinary" call to it, and that they were therefore required by God to preach. Wesley replied, "Methodism is an extraordinary dispensation of His Providence. Therefore I do not wonder if several things occur therein which do not fall under ordinary rules of discipline."[17] Not only were the circumstances extraordinary, but reading Schmidt's account of the specific women of American Methodism, one cannot help but think that many were truly extraordinary. From Jarena Lee, an African American woman preacher who preached to racially mixed congregations as early as the 1820s, to Belle Harris Bennett, the first woman to address the General Conference of 1910, even though they would not seat her as a delegate, Schmidt's history recounts the lives of amazing women. When put into their sociohistorical contexts, we might describe them as the right women at the right time.

Schmidt's main sources were memoirs, diaries and letters, written by these women as they reflected on their lives. Joanna Bowen Gillespie, an important secondary source for Schmidt, notes that these documents "exhibit a newly emerging sense of female self-empowerment, religiously sanctioned."[18] That is, as women found their own voices as independent, intelligent actors in a world previously closed to them, they described God as leading them in new ways. Stepping out into the public arena, even if limiting their focus to making the world home-like or other work more appropriate to women, it was God's call that they felt urging them on—not merely their own desires. Theological teachings and religious rhetoric provided the language through which they began to understand and define themselves anew.

The development of identity in social context is an important aspect of sociological imagination. These women's stories are not only told to maintain the historical record of who said what and when, but they are also told as a testimony to women's changing sense of themselves as they struggled with the old models of womanhood and replaced them with new.

Many of these women wrote about wanting to be "useful." As Methodists, they were required to attend meetings at which they reported to others about their ongoing progress toward perfection. The main thrust of this project was not supposed to be based on personal efforts, but on submission to God's grace. At the same time, these early Methodists were very busy, dedicating time to prayer, study, works of mercy, and exhortation of others. John Wesley's mother, Susanna, was one of the first. In a letter to her husband, she wrote, "Though I am not a man, nor a minister

17. Wesley, *The Letters*, 257.

18. Gillespie, *The Clear Leadings of Providence*, 198.

of the gospel, and so cannot be employed in such a worthy employment as they were, yet . . . I might do somewhat more than I do. I thought I might live in a more exemplary manner . . . I resolved to begin with my own children."[19] She then explained her method of meeting with each child one night a week to talk about individual concerns, which was something she considered important for any good mother. She did not limit herself to her children though—she merely "began" there. Just a few lines later, she reported reading sermons to "those few neighbors who then came to me . . . Last Sunday, I believe we had above two hundred, and yet many went away for want of room."[20]

Susanna's path to perfection included not just self reflection, but a fairly public ministry. And as she struggled with her role as a woman, she responded to complaints that she was overstepping her bounds. When her husband suggested that she let someone else do the reading, she responded that there was no one else literate enough to read well, nor anyone with a voice strong enough to be heard. Because of these skills, she felt she was uniquely qualified to serve as an instrument of God, despite the criticisms of others, and even her personal desires. It is hard, if not impossible to read these accounts through twenty-first-century feminist eyes. Was Susanna truly submitting to what she thought was God's will, or was she enjoying the public and powerful role of preacher while her husband, their regular pastor, was away? I would like to think it was a bit of both, but regardless of what was in her mind, it was through religion that Susanna was able to step into a new role for women, something that was not lost on her son, who just a few years later would sanction women preachers because of the positive results of their work. Whether or not women enjoyed their work or not, they clearly saw it as the work of God, and themselves as merely God's instruments.

Over what is now almost three centuries of Methodism, a number of similarly extraordinary Methodist women made comparable pleas in regard to an expansion of women's roles, roles to which they felt called by God. In each chapter of her book, Schmidt briefly summarizes the stories of some of them, describing her accounts as "intimate portraits."[21] Although they are intimate in that they share aspects of personal life that

19. Wallace, *Susanna Wesley*, 80.
20. Ibid.
21. Schmidt, *Grace Sufficient*, 20.

we might consider quite private today, at the time, many were considerably well known as a kind of Methodist lore—stories of faith meant to inspire that same faith in others. One popular genre of early Methodism was the death memoir, published in the *Methodist Magazine,* and more commonly written by women than men. Life was precarious in many ways, and health care was minimal, so people usually died at home, surrounded by family members and friends who later bore witness to the event. The chance of dying in childbirth was high, so many pregnant women prepared their burial plans and expressed concern about their spiritual state throughout the pregnancy. For Methodists, these last opportunities to attest to their faith represented just another step in their path to perfection. They could communicate to others that they were not afraid to die and exhort others to prepare to eventually meet them in heaven. Schmidt recounts that one woman told her audience of fellow Methodists to continue to attend their class meetings, and another exhorted her husband to lift a burden that had been on her mind by releasing his slaves.[22] It was through these testimonies that women could feel useful, right up to the end of their lives, and in many ways, continue the public ministries to which they were becoming accustomed.

Another new "field of usefulness"[23] was the role of minister's wife. Although Protestants had officially abandoned required celibacy for clergy years ago as part of the Reformation, early Methodist preachers were always on the move, itinerating over hundreds of miles of territory to serve congregations across the American frontier. As a result, the vast majority were young, poor, and single. Those who chose to "locate" by settling down in one place and preaching only locally had to leave the itinerant status. Some early leaders felt this would jeopardize the growth of the movement, so it was initially discouraged.[24] However, the increasingly institutionalized denomination began to demand a higher educated clergy, which meant increasingly middle class and more settled—at least not constantly on the move. With that came a new opportunity for women, and indeed, a new religious vocation: the minister's wife.

These early clergy wives had hard lives, and many aspects of their stories read like dreadful tales of sheer endurance. Mary Orne Tucker

22. Ibid., 48.
23. Ibid., 116.
24. Ibid., 114.

travelled over 160 miles with her husband to the various churches in his Vermont charge, riding two on one horse and boarding in log huts along the way. In 1858 Oregon, Rebecca Fisher prevented an outbreak of mob violence before a camp meeting, boldly stepping up and telling the ring leader that he should "behave himself."[25] Catherine Paine Blaine travelled by mule, steamer, and then Indian canoe, to reach her new parsonage in Washington. Once there, she took up the more typical woman's work of cleaning the church, but was known to complain about how careless the people were in caring for it, and that she had to clean up after muddy shoes, and even worse, after the tobacco juice spit by members of the congregation.[26] Another unnamed minster's wife reported that she would never answer the door of the parsonage without her revolver in her hand.[27]

It was not only the demands of the frontier, but also those of the itinerant ministry, that invited women to take up more traditionally "masculine" tasks. Minister's wives, in the style of Susanna Wesley, were often asked to read sermons to the congregation in the absence of the pastor, who regularly had to travel to distant outposts in service to other churches. Wives also organized missionary societies to raise money for missionary efforts, which involved public speaking, financial accounting, advertising, and other business-related duties. According to Schmidt, these clergy wives rose to the challenge specifically because they sensed a call from God to do extraordinary work under challenging circumstances. Their amazing biographies attest to the power of individual women in shaping Methodism on the frontier. The frontier context of near-constant struggle was faced by women who, like Frances Merritt said, "I feared my weak nerves could not endure such powerful tonics," yet they did.[28]

Because macro, meso and micro elements in a good historical analysis cannot be explained without reference to each other, it is difficult to disentangle the separate parts. Individual women like Anna Howard Shaw and Anna Oliver, the first women to apply for ordination in the Methodist Episcopal Church, might not have sought clergy rights if other women had not been preaching for years, partly due to necessity in a quickly growing movement, but also because of a radical Methodist ideology that

25. Ibid., 125.
26. Ibid., 127.
27. Ibid., 129.
28. Ibid.

privileged experience over tradition. Women like Frances Willard might not have sought new arenas of usefulness if they had not encountered a theology that expected so much of them as religious actors in pursuit of perfection and especially in an era of early American expansive notions of equality. All of these elements are inextricably linked in a complicated dance of social forces, the whole of which must be included in one's analysis to understand the past as well as the present, and so as to plan for the future. It is to the present and future to which we now turn.

## The Contemporary Church: Agents in Social Contexts

Like the people in Schmidt's history, contemporary United Methodists are living in dynamic and noteworthy social contexts. In order to understand the ubiquitous social forces that both empower and delimit human activities, it is important to see both the Methodist movement of the past and the United Methodist Church of the present as living, not only through individual leaders, but through and within complicated times. Let us look at two examples of sites where contemporary United Methodism is facing changing social contexts in terms of its message and its structure. It may be in understanding these intersections that church leaders can best plan for a future that will capitalize on the needs of its times, as opposed to fighting against the forces of the inevitable. Time marches on, and from Schmidt's account, it seems that the innovative women of American Methodism's first two centuries jumped into that parade of industrialization, urbanization, abolition and feminism wherever they could, eventually finding themselves and their movement/church in prominent positions in American society, and seeing it as the work of God. What does that parade look like today, and are Methodists jumping into the mix, or simply ignoring the social contexts as they pass us by?

First, let us look at the message of Methodism. Few people would argue with Schmidt and others who say that the original message of Methodism was radically egalitarian. It appealed, not to the upper classes and powerful in society, but to the poor, to slaves, and to women. The demands of disciplined Methodist practice gave marginalized people a way to form an identity of self-worth and a path toward a life of fulfilling usefulness. Wealthy white men already had both, so they did not need to become Methodists, often joining begrudgingly, or only at the urging of their mothers and wives. Even outside of Methodism, women have always been the majority of participants in American religion. Perhaps it is the general message of hope, or the supportive community that most religions provide, but people on the margins have always found a home in religion, at least more so than their wealthier counterparts, for whom life seems more secure.

Is that demanding discipline still at the center of Methodism today, and if it is heard at all, into what context? The answer to the first question is no. The demands of the early class meetings and bands, requiring weekly and sometimes more frequent attendance at meetings with small groups of like-minded others, have long been abandoned. The radical Methodist movement has grown into a fully mature institution, now as concerned with business items like budgets and ordination procedures as with spiritual life and the relief of human suffering. There is no one to blame—it is simply the inevitable result of institutionalization—the unintended consequence of the "success" of growth.

The best contemporary comparison with those early gatherings may be Alcoholics Anonymous. In both settings people tell their stories, give each other encouragement for the next days, and then they hold one another accountable for attempting to complete their goals. Because they were marginalized, the early Methodists knew they couldn't live counterculturally alone, and they needed support. Although they did not articulate it this way, early Methodists saw the path to perfection as lived one day at a time, and they constantly turned to one another to make it through the next day.

Today, alcoholics and others with addiction-related problems regularly attend AA and other twelve-step-program meetings, some of which are held in United Methodist churches— ironically, the perfect place for such a meeting. Meetings of American United Methodists, on the other hand, are on the decline. Not only are membership numbers down and falling, but even those who do remain are much more marginal participants than their predecessors. But that is the nature of movements over institutions. Movements thrive on demanding membership requirements, on expelling people for breaches of the rules, on making it hard, but exciting to participate. Marginalized people often flock to such groups, which give them a sense of meaning and a feeling of belonging to something vital. Paradoxically though, when the message is truly compelling, the desire to share it is intense, and as more and more people join and the group becomes diverse, it also becomes less unified, and most importantly, less committed. Leadership is delegated to a few, and the average member does less and less. And as the message becomes more palatable and less demanding, the group becomes less edgy and more mainstream, eventually attractive even to the upper classes. Eventually, membership is no longer a countercultural statement, but a mark of respectability. Today, no one would hesitate to ask someone where s/he goes to church, and similarly, no one would hesitate to say s/he was United Methodist. But the choice is simple, and not really a choice at all—either grow into an institution, or die the slow death of a movement/sect. Remaining in the state of a protest (we too soon forget the roots of the term *Protestant*) movement is too demanding for most people over time, so the pressure to institutionalize is virtually inevitable.

Many United Methodists today yearn for that vital movement of the past, the one with a radical countercultural message that would attract and serve the marginalized of the world. The mistake is in looking to individuals outside of social contexts to make it happen. What did the women of Schmidt's history have that we don't have? Nothing, but they lived in different sociohistorical contexts. Some of the early Methodists may have been truly extraordinary, but more often they were simply able to understand and respond to the opportunities of their times. What does the contemporary context mean for today's United Methodists?

Perhaps the well established, and now declining institution, can be revitalized just as it once revitalized the Church of England—through a radical countercultural reform movement. Some see themselves as poised for this—groups such as the Confessing Movement (pro–traditional Trinitarian theology) on the right, or the Reconciling Congregations Movement (pro-GLBT-inclusive theology) on the left, the first stressing the radical movement message that heretics should be expelled, and the other stressing the equally radical movement message that the marginalized are truly welcome—both beliefs of the early Methodists. Unfortunately, neither of these groups has caught on with the fervor of the early Methodists, partly because there are other contextual factors missing today, such as the novelty of the democratic American experiment of equality—the perfect soil for the growth of a radically egalitarian movement. Also, the United Methodist Church is now a well established institution, more like the Church of England of Wesley's day than the radial movement he inspired.

Much about the social context is also different today. Religious belief in the United States remains high, but religious practice, especially through large-scale institutions, is on the wane.[29] Personal affirmations of faith are strong, but the public practice of religion has been declining since the early 1970s. For many, religion has become more an interesting individualized and part-time hobby of spiritual self-fulfillment, rather than an integral part of identity and social life. In contrast, shopping centers never close, the average home is larger than ever, and at least one entire television channel is dedicated solely to reporting on the economy and the stock market, signs that the pursuit of material comfort has become more important than the pursuit of holiness.

But developing demanding new Methodist movements seems unlikely. It is the marginalized who initiate and join such movements, not the middle class. Such movements tend to be attractive to those who are marginalized, while most American United Methodists are members of the middle class with much to lose by challenging the status quo. As one concrete example, United Methodist Bishops now make more than twice the salary of the median American family—not exactly the sign of a spiritual organization in solidarity with the poor. To be fair though, most clergy salaries are small, and United Methodists regularly spend millions of dollars on ongoing aid and emergency relief all over the world. Unfortunately though, it costs a lot to run a large organization, whether church or for profit, and the difference between CEOs' salaries and those of ordinary workers is increasing across the board. Similarly, the most recent General Conference gathering, the two week long quadrennial meeting at which the denomination revises its Book of Discipline and rededicates itself to the mission and various projects of the church, cost about six million dollars. Just the cost of doing business? Maybe, but it's hard to convert a highly structured institution into a radical, countercultural social movement.

Wesley himself, however charismatic he may have been, did not transform an institution into a movement; instead he stood up to the comparable institution of his day and gave it hell, so to speak. He went against the rules, allowed women to preach, ordained otherwise unauthorized preachers for America, and called people to radical lifestyles that were not respected in the churches or the larger society of his day. And while ultimately, his critique of the Church of England may have positively impacted Anglicanism, primarily he inspired a radical movement,

29. Altemeyer, "The Decline of Organized Religion," 79.

which has now become a mainstream denomination. In those days, to be called "Methodist" was not a compliment—it was a derogatory term used to make fun of people who seemed to be crazily seeking holiness through almost constant focus on God (through Bible study and mutual accountability groups) and serving others (through simplifying one's lifestyle, tithing, and acts of mercy). Today, to be called a "Methodist" may not be exactly a compliment, but it is not an insult either. It is a thoroughly socially acceptable association, no longer countercultural, but completely in sync with the larger society. The contemporary United Methodist Church has become exactly the kind of institution that Wesley tried to reform. This is crucial to understanding the status of United Methodism today.

So the original radical message will no longer work in what is now an institutionalized church. Schmidt and others have referred to this aspect of the history of American Methodism as the movement from "side street to Main Street."[30] Sociological evidence shows that such transitions as Methodism experienced lead to moderation of the message for the sake of social respectability. Wesley was aware of this tendency of religious revival to fizzle. Sociologist Max Weber quoted Wesley in his classic, *The Protestant Ethic and the Spirit of Capitalism*: "I fear, where riches have increased, the essence of religion has decreased in the same proportion. Therefore, I do not see how it is possible, in the nature of things, for any revival of true religion to continue long."[31] It is simply the nature of radical social movements to grow or die. And if they grow, they become rich and thereby lose the very thing that made them compelling. That is the reality for the contemporary church, a contextual factor that must be included in an analysis of how to move into the future.

If the original message will no longer work, what about the structure? One of the hallmarks of Methodist organization, from its start to the present, is the itineracy—the regular assignment of clergy to pastoral charges, as determined by the resident (also itinerant) Bishop in consultation with the District Superintendents appointed to serve the Annual Conference. In Wesley's day, this was fairly easy, as he and a small group of his assistants were able to oversee the assignments throughout England, and even some of the first in America. Francis Asbury, one of the earliest and most important leaders of American Methodism, was able to do the

---

30. Schmidt, *Grace Sufficient*, 151.
31. Weber, *The Protestant Ethic*, 175.

same in the United States, also with a little help and a lot of travel. After his death in 1816, membership increased dramatically, and by the middle of the century, numbered more than 1.7 million.[32] The current church, spanning four continents, numbers over eleven million members, and employs about 50 Bishops to oversee over 45,000 ordained clergy in the United States alone. Suffice to say, the appointment and relocation of United Methodist clergy is a complicated endeavor on the macro, or denominational scale, and also on the micro scale, that is, for each church and each clergyperson. The developments around itinerancy are interesting, but too complicated to discuss here, so let us simply focus on one aspect of the contemporary situation in today's social context.

Recently, the United Methodist Commission on the Status and Role of Women study on clergy spouses and families showed itinerancy to be the most problematic aspect of life in the ministry for spouses, noted ahead of the heavy time demands, financial struggles, and living in neglected parsonages. Most felt that their personal concerns and especially their jobs were not considered important to the church, and therefore they felt that they were ignored in appointment decisions. Interestingly, both male and female spouses felt that their careers were not valued as much as the careers of spouses of the other sex.[33] There is also plenty of popular Methodist lore about the difficulties of moving for the children of clergy, but this study polled only spouses.

The frequent and distant reassignment of single, low-paid men did not pose a challenge to the small radical Methodist movement, but in a modern institutionalized denomination with married clergy of both sexes, there are challenges. First, marriage itself became acceptable for Methodist clergy, and eventually, they and their families wanted to stop moving and settle down. In the early days and up until the second half of the twentieth century, there was still a lot of movement of clergy, but with only male clergy and homemaker/wives as spouses, it was relatively easy to pick up and move to a new place. Today, clergy are both male and female, and the great majority of all spouses work outside the home, so moving poses new problems for clergy families. If the United Methodist Church wants to limit ordination to single people or those with stay-at-home spouses, the traditional system might continue to work, but in the

32. Norwood, *The Story of American Methodism*, 259.
33. Murphy-Geiss, *Clergy Spouses*, 17.

contemporary context of dual-career couples and the popularity of marriage (90% of Americans marry at least once[34]), that limitation is neither likely nor desirable.

Taking these two areas of message and structure together, and using a sociological imagination as the basis for analysis, the contemporary church leader must first assess whether the United Methodist Church wants to claim its roots and re-radicalize into a movement, or accept its status as an established and moderate denomination. If the first, membership would be small and requirements demanding. In fact, much would have to change, but the itinerancy of clergy would be simplified. There is certainly a precedent for that kind of focus in the history of Methodism; indeed, Methodism first thrived in response to a moderate church much like the one it has become. If the latter, the message can remain more moderate and the demands on members can be small, but the itinerancy will have to adjust, as new clergy are likely to be married to working spouses whose careers matter to them, and whose incomes may be important as the main breadwinners of the family.

Understanding the denomination (mesolevel) in the social context of movement to church and changing gender/family roles (macrolevel) and how all of those things impact individuals is essential in getting the full picture of what has been and what might be ahead for any organization. Historians like Schmidt can help us more fully understand the past in covering all of those levels and the interconnections between them. It is in reading Schmidt's work that we can grasp the exciting times of the early movement as well as the transition from side street to Main Street that brought us to today. In looking to the future, church leaders will have to understand those dynamics as well, applying the same rich, multilevel, sociological imagination to present sociohistoric contexts. Can the contemporary United Methodist Church again be a radical force for holiness in a relatively wealthy, individualistic, and secular society? Or must it admit the "success" of past growth, and accept its fate as a moderate denomination, serving others the best it can while also serving itself, a large and bureaucratic organization of largely upper-middle-class members whose idea of holiness is no longer radical, but more suitable for Main Street, America, where it came to be lodged? Or can some middle ground be created, a church of radical holiness, but practiced by many, and not limited by the constraints of institutionalization that come with

34. Cherlin, *The Marriage-Go-Round*, 4.

growth? A rich sociological imagination is required to envision a future Methodism that is intentional in its direction, and not simply driven by the ubiquitous and all but inevitable social forces.

## BIBLIOGRAPHY

Altemeyer, Bob. "The Decline of Organized Religion in Western Civilization." *The International Journal for the Psychology of Religion* 14/2 (2004) 77–89.

Chaves, Mark. *Ordaining Women: Culture and Conflict in Religious Organizations.* Cambridge: Harvard University Press, 1997.

Cherlin, Andrew. *The Marriage-Go-Round: The State of Marriage and the Family in America Today.* New York: Vintage, 2009.

Gaustad, Edwin S. *A Religious History of America.* New York: Harper & Row, 1966.

Gifford, Carolyn De Swarte, editor. *Writing Out My Heart: Selections from the Journal of Frances E. Willard 1855–96.* Urbana: University of Illinois Press, 1995.

Gillespie, Joanna Bowen. "'The Clear Leadings of Providence': Pious Memoirs and the Problems of Self-Realization for Women in the Early Nineteenth Century." *Journal of the Early Republic* 5 (Summer 1985) 197–221.

Johnstone, Ronald L. *Religion in Society: A Sociology of Religion.* 8th ed. Upper Saddle River, NJ: Pearson/Prentice Hall, 2007.

Lindley, Susan Hill. *"You Have Stept Out of Your Place": A History of Women and Religion in America.* Louisville: Westminster John Knox, 1996.

Mills, C. Wright. *The Sociological Imagination.* Oxford: Oxford University Press, 2000.

Murphy-Geiss, Gail E. "Clergy Spouses and Families in the United Methodist Church, Part II: Local Church Expectations and What Clergy Spouses Most Want the UMC to Know." Chicago: General Commission on the Status and Role of Women, United Methodist Church, 2009.

Norwood, Frederick A. *The Story of American Methodism: A History of the United Methodists and Their Relations.* Nashville: Abingdon, 1974.

Schmidt, Jean Miller. *Grace Sufficient: A History of Women in American Methodism 1760–1939.* Nashville: Abingdon, 1999.

Wallace, Charles, Jr., editor. *Susanna Wesley: The Complete Writings.* New York: Oxford University Press, 1997.

Weber, Max. *The Protestant Ethic and the Spirit of Capitalism.* London: Routledge, 1992.

Wesley, John. *The Letters of the Rev. John Wesley.* Vol. 5, *Feb 28, 1766 to Dec. 9, 1772.* Edited by John Telford. London: Epworth, 1931.

Willard, Frances E. "How to Win: A Book for Girls." In *Let Something Good Be Said: Speeches and Writings of Frances E. Willard,* edited by Carolyn DeSwarte Gifford and Amy R. Slagell, 100–116. Urbana: University of Illinois Press, 2007.

# Pastoral Response

## Elaine Stanovsky

### Still Sufficient Grace

C AN AN ESTABLISHED CHURCH experience the freshness and innovation of a reform movement? Dr. Murphy-Geiss leads us to the heart of the challenge facing The United Methodist Church today. Must the Church choose between being a high-commitment, countercultural movement or a low-commitment, mainstream cultural institution? What leadership does the church need for its ministry to be faithful and fruitful?

I find the answer to Murphy-Geiss's questions in Jean Miller Schmidt's affirmation that people of faith hear and follow the "extraordinary call" of God even when the church fails to recognize or embrace it.[1] Schmidt demonstrates the specific example of women in early Methodism who were empowered by the gospel of Jesus Christ, long before established churches embraced their leadership gifts.

As I read the interplay of biography, history, and social science in Schmidt's treasury of women's lives, I also listen for the ways the biblical narrative intersects their stories. Might the rise of Methodism as a movement and the rise of women into leadership within the Methodist movement bear marks of the biblical story? Might that same biblical story offer hope for our present challenge? How might "biblical imagination"[2]

---

1. Schmidt, *Grace Sufficient.*
2. Roxburgh and Romanuk, *The Missional Leader.*

as described by the missional church movement lead us to fresh and innovative engagement of the gospel with the real lives of people and communities in ways that awaken the church from its dormancy?

I claim the Methodist movement as a work of the Holy Spirit in the lives of individuals at a particular time and place in history. I also claim, with Jean Miller Schmidt, the rise of women to leadership both inside and outside the church as a work of the Holy Spirit in the context of historical and social realities. And I believe that the Holy Spirit is working today in the lives of people both inside and outside the structures of the church, encouraging new forms and expressions of Christian faithfulness that will serve present realities of history and society.

High commitment and high demand describe the *method* of early *Method*ists, who were expected to join, attend, study, pray, answer, examine, witness, visit, and give. Their participation was counted and reported. They gave account of their lives and received counsel. But the *method* was the means to the end of forming Christian disciples who believed they played an important part in God's mission to the world. They constantly examined and reformed their lives in the light of Christian Scripture and prayer.

The *method* led people to "extraordinary calls." John Wesley ventured into prisons and poor houses, factories, and fields at a time when the Church of England thought ministry occurred within church buildings. Frances Willard heard a call to ministry at a time when the church did not know how to use her gifts. "But even my dear old mother-church (the Methodist) did not call women to her altars. I was too timid to go without a call; and so it came about that while my unconstrained preference would long ago have led me to the pastorate, I have failed of it."[3] The closed doors of the church did not stop her. She followed her call to a life of advocacy on behalf of women and children, and against slavery, domestic violence and drunkenness, on the margins of the church through the Women's Christian Temperance Movement.

If we believe the gospel message that new life arises out of defeat and death, then who are we to give up on the church? The church today is full of people who read the Bible and ask, "What does this story have to do with my life, with the world?" In every age the Holy Spirit issues new "extraordinary calls" to a new generation of disciples who go where they

---

3. Willard, *Woman in the Pulpit*, 62.

are sent—not where they have been invited—because the gospel empowers them to be more than they have ever been or imagined they could be. They transcend their upbringing, their training, their fear, to carry the gospel to places the institutional church is not agile to go.

The health and vitality of the Methodist tradition lies in its confidence that if we lead people into relationship with the Holy Spirit, they will be transformed, and will become agents of creative transformation.[4] Their transformative work will not be limited to the spiritual lives of individuals. It will also transform the church and the world. In this way, the very message of the gospel of Jesus Christ carries the source of renewal and regeneration of the church.

An institutionalized church threatens this tendency toward innovation by creating systems of accountability and control that can stifle the fresh leadings of the Holy Spirit. Murphy-Geiss warns that the church may be so deeply stuck in its policies and procedures that it can no longer follow the leading of the Holy Spirit to adapt to new circumstances. She implies that there is a danger that the church will be stronger than the gospel; that ecclesial systems of control and conservatism will constrain the work of the Holy Spirit. I'm not afraid. The Holy Spirit will not be stopped from descending to touch and change people in our day inside the church as well as outside. I am encouraged by the many faithful within the church who search the night skies for new stars that mark the hope of the future and who uproot, journey, witness, praise, share, and serve God's continuing revelation and guidance in our day.

Key to successful adaptation of the church today is recovery of two dormant roots of our tradition. First, church life and especially new ministry will find strength in small covenant groups for spiritual growth and accountability. This is where faith emerges and where spirits stretch to new limits. Second, faithfulness will spread by empowered laity who once again carry the gospel into their everyday lives and become the invitational gatherers of new faith communities. These two elements of our tradition underlie the egalitarianism and reductionism Murphy-Geiss suggests were central to the strength of the early Methodist movement.

As one who faces the challenges and enjoys the benefits of an established church, my mission is to cultivate creative transformation within the church. I live in confidence that if we work the *method,* introducing

4. Cobb, *Christ in a Pluralistic Age.*

people to the gospel, nurturing them in small covenant communities of accountability, sending them out as disciple-missionaries to their friends and neighbors with gospel and grace that transforms lives, God's mission will take root and the church will bear fruit.

Jean Miller Schmidt reveals that God has been faithful through the extraordinary lives of people of faith in the past. God is faithful today. It is the Church's challenge to recognize and affirm the Holy Spirit's holy presence in people who carry the gospel in new ways and to new people. Where does my confidence come from? Biblical imagination, informed by an empty tomb and the remarkable testimony of my foremothers that there is grace sufficient to the challenge.

Grace is still sufficient.

## BIBLIOGRAPHY

Cobb, John B., Jr. *Christ in a Pluralistic Age*. Philadelphia: Westminster, 1975.

Roxburgh, Alan J., and Fred Romanuk. *The Missional Leader: Equipping Your Church to Reach a Changing World*. San Francisco: Jossey-Bass, 2006.

Schmidt, Jean Miller. *Grace Sufficient: A History of Women in American Methodism, 1760–1939*. Nashville: Abingdon, 1999.

Willard, Frances E. *Woman in the Pulpit*. Boston: Lothrop, 1888.

# Chapter Two

## Inclusive Ecclesiology
### A New Model of Hospitality

### Deborah Beth Creamer

VISITORS WELCOME! EVERYONE WELCOME! Church message boards and bulletins proclaim invitation; congregations describe themselves as places that are open to strangers, neighbors, and guests. Even the present campaign of the United Methodist Church—"open hearts, open minds, open doors"—paints a picture of inclusive ecclesiology, a vision of church where all are welcome. While this may be our stated ideal, and even our genuine hope, we cannot deny that there are those whom we do not genuinely welcome, those who, intentionally or not, we leave outside the gate. Perhaps sometimes each of us finds ourselves left outside, unable to fully join with community in the way we might desire. This chapter takes as its starting point the biblical mandate of hospitality, particularly the image from Luke 14:13—"when you give a banquet, invite the poor, the crippled, the lame, and the blind"—to imagine what it might look like to struggle together toward a genuinely inclusive ecclesiology, a community space where everyone is welcome.

The word *ecclesiology* comes from the Greek *ekklēsia*, "church," and *logos*, "study," and so it means, quite simply, the study of the church. Musser and Price describe it as "the church's understanding of its own existence."[1] This is, necessarily, a theological (as well as sociological, historical, and practical) undertaking. Ecclesiology takes us beyond the sense of church as a physical building or a social club and reminds us that church is anywhere two or three are gathered in Jesus's name (Matt 18:20). Ecclesiology also looks at the ways in which church functions as "a sign of the coming fulfillment of God's promise for new creation."[2] It is a place where we can imagine, experiment, and strive for more than we can presently accomplish. Church is both a now and a not-yet, a space of who we are in this moment as well as a sign of who we wish to be. Thus ecclesiology, as the theological study of church, must also be concerned with both who we are and who we strive to become. For this reason, Russell and Clarkson describe ecclesiology as not a static undertaking or a one-time project but rather an ongoing process by which "the church rethinks the meaning of its self-understanding as a community of Jesus Christ in every changing circumstance."[3] The work of ecclesiology—the examination, critique, and re-imagination of who we can be as church—is never done.

One of the places where this re-imagination has occurred, and continues to occur, is around the presence and challenges posed by women who seek to have their voices heard and their gifts acknowledged within traditional church structures, as, for example, narrated in the diaries, letters, and other accounts preserved for us by historians like Jean Miller Schmidt. The challenges posed by these women have changed the church, particularly as they have not simply requested a place at a pre-set table but, at least in some ways, have changed the furnishings and structures to their core.[4] From this endeavor, we see that the church cannot become more inclusive by simply inviting "them" to join "us;" rather, we must be open to the risk of change and the vulnerability that comes with genuine hospitality.

1. Musser and Price, *New Handbook*, 135.

2. Russell and Clarkson, *Dictionary*, 75.

3. Ibid., 74–75.

4. See, for example, the discussion of new models in the form of roundtable connection, kitchen-table solidarity, and welcome-table partnership in Russell, *Church in the Round*; or Thistlethwaite and Engel's observation that these projects "are not about rearranging the furniture in the house of theology, or even about redecorating or remodeling the house. Rather, they are about rebuilding the foundation (method) and redesigning the floor plan (categories)" (*Lift Every Voice*, 14).

This chapter will explore another category of people who often do not find welcome within our churches. Individuals with disabilities often experience significant barriers in our communities and congregations, sometimes due to physical and architectural impediments (a flight of stairs, an outdated sound system) but perhaps more often due to obstacles that come from attitudes about disability. Attention to disability as an issue of genuine hospitality allows us to consider ways to become more accessible to those who presently experience a lack of welcome and also offers an access point to how we might think about issues of inclusion and exclusion more broadly.[5] The chapter will begin with a brief introduction to the experience of disability, and then will move into theological reflections on what it would look like to consider disability as a normal experience and even as part of the goodness of creation. From this foundation of a recognition and respect for human limits, the chapter will then explore images of God that resonate with this experience and invite even broader notions of inclusion. As we will see, images that we find in disability offer notions of church that allow us to propose an inclusive ecclesiology that does not see hospitality as a false welcoming of "the other" but rather recognizes and affirms the presence of diversity, breaks down false dichotomies, and affirms the distinctiveness and fundamental value of each of us within God's creation.

## Disability and Inclusion

According to the Census Bureau, 18 percent of the people in the United States have some sort of disability, and 12 percent have what is considered a severe disability, meaning that they are unable to perform certain tasks without assistance from a person or a device.[6] Since this comes to more than one in ten people, or two in seven families,[7] it makes sense then that most of us would know at least one person with a significant disability, whether that be a member of our family, a close friend, or someone from work or school or church—or, perhaps, even, ourself. The familiarity of disability becomes even more obvious when we think about continuum

5. Similar analyses could be taken in relation to other identity categories, such as race, ethnicity, or GLBTQ status; for the sake of this chapter, I will intentionally limit this queering of categories to the lens of disability.

6. *Americans with Disabilities:* 2005.

7. Ibid.

of disability: each of us has or has had some experiences that are similar to disability, whether using eyeglasses to help us read more easily, recognizing that the absence of curb cuts is a problem when pushing a stroller or laundry cart, negotiating the world on crutches after breaking a leg or spraining an ankle, or having a sore hip or knee that acts up when the weather changes. Disability is not some foreign category but rather is something that we are all familiar with, to some extent or another. Finally, disability can be called an "open minority," meaning that it is a category or identity that anyone can join at any point—tomorrow, anyone who is not disabled could become disabled, anyone who is disabled could become differently disabled, and anyone who has some form of disability today could find that condition improved or worsened tomorrow. As the Census Bureau observes, frequency and severity of disability increases as the population ages.[8] All this reminds us that disability is not some strange and foreign concept. Rather, it is very close to home, literally and figuratively, and thus it is somewhat surprising that religious communities do not discuss it or attend to it more often than they do.

As interesting as it is to be reminded that disability is far more common than we tend to notice, this is not the only way to highlight the importance of inclusion. For Christians, as for people of other faith traditions, there are clearly stated obligations to include others: to invite the blind, crippled, and lame (Luke 14:13); to do unto the least of these (Matt 25:40); to do unto others (Matt 7:12). The parables of the lost sheep (Matt 18:10–14) and of the lost coin (Luke 15:8–10) remind us that even a single lost one is worth our attention. Beyond these theological claims, there is also a pragmatic argument based on the fact that people with disabilities are an untapped resource, a population underserved by church (and other) communities.[9] If a church is looking to increase its membership numbers or its donor base, it might well consider ways to reach out to the more than 54 million people with disabilities in the United States alone.[10]

Yet this sense of including the other as "other," or, on the other hand, as "just like us," is insufficient if what we desire is a truly inclusive ecclesiology. As both Scripture and the traditions of the church teach us, genuine hospitality is not a false welcoming of the "other" on our terms

8. Ibid.

9. Harris Interactive, "Kessler Foundation." Online: http://www.2010disabilitysurveys.org/.

10. *Americans with Disabilities:* 2005.

but instead includes the recognition and affirmation of diversity, breaking down false dichotomies between "us" and "them" and asserting the fundamental inherent value of each of us within the story of God's creation. This means that we must go further than just including people with disabilities into "our" space—for example, cutting out part of a pew so that someone in a wheelchair can join the congregation in the sanctuary—but rather working together from a multitude of perspectives to create spaces that truly seek to be inclusive.

A first step is to recognize that we are often limited by our own stereotypes and preconceptions: we simply do not see the ways in which we are excluding another. While moving beyond our embedded assumptions can be a long and difficult process, one way to begin is simply by paying attention, or what Sallie McFague calls "attention epistemology."[11] At one level, this simply means noticing everyday things that you might not have noticed before: signs on the bus that say "wheelchairs have priority" (rather than, "*people* in wheelchairs have priority"), a curb cut located a significant distance from handicapped parking spaces and the building entrance, an automated door where the button is out of reach or blocked by a flowerpot or garbage can, and so on. It also means noticing when an advertisement includes a TTD/TTY number, or when the aisles in a grocery store are wide enough for scooters to navigate comfortably, or when libraries have large-print books indicated by a large-print sign. In congregations, it means, not only noticing the presence or absence of elevators and assistive listening devices, but also recognizing whether communion services are accessible to all and whether the congregation has found comfortable phrasing to replace "please stand." Beyond looking at practical issues, it can also involve asking what it means to engage theology from the perspective of disability, and particularly how experiences of disability might contribute to our images and understandings of God. Trying on this sort of "lens of disability" can allow one to broaden one's perspective about both present situations and future possibilities and is a proactive step one can take in addition to engaging in conversation with people with various disabilities about these same issues.

It is important to note, of course, that the lens of disability (or the experience of having a disability, or of being labeled as a person with a disability) does not lead to a single unified perspective. There is a huge

11. McFague, *Body of God*, 49.

diversity in the sorts of experiences that are considered to be a "disability." It is problematic to assume that people who use wheelchairs automatically have much in common with people who communicate through sign language or with those who do not rely on short-term memory. It is problematic to even assume that people who use wheelchairs have much in common with each other, just by virtue of that wheelchair. Our use of labels sometimes hides the fact that these can be dramatically different experiences. The physical experience itself may be quite different: we live in distinctly different bodies and have unique reactions to and experiences in those bodies. Some people experience disability as suffering or loss; others see it as an intrinsic part of their own identity. Some people experience disability as primarily an experience of physical impairment; others encounter it largely as an experience of social exclusion or prejudice.[12] And beyond that, it is important to remember that people with disabilities hold widely divergent opinions and views about life more broadly. As Susan Brooks Thistlethwaite and Mary Potter Engel remark, "people look alike only when you cannot be bothered to look at them closely."[13] This is true theologically as well. Some people with disabilities do not believe in God at all. Others believe in a very active or powerful God. Some struggle with God; others are comfortable in their faith. We cannot simply talk about "what people with disabilities believe about God" any more than we could make a single claim about "what people without disabilities believe about God." However, we can reflect on experiences of disability and then explore how these experiences might contribute to our images of God.

It is important to note that the attempt here is not to describe or even suggest what or who God "is." Scripture and tradition describe for us a God who is beyond human understanding or categories, as well as One whom we each encounter out of our unique locations and experiences. Rather, I draw here on the perspective offered by Sallie McFague, who suggests that all religious language is metaphorical and so the theologian is charged with the task of using "the best images available to us in order to say something about the divine."[14] Our task, then, is to find or create

12. A fuller discussion of the two prominent models for disability, the medical and the minority/social model, is beyond the scope of this essay. For more on these models, how they function and their common critiques, see Creamer, *Disability and Christian Theology*, 22–33.

13. Thistlethwaite and Engel, *Lift Every Voice*, 3.

14. McFague, "Earthly Theological Agenda," 2.

these "best" images, while still recognizing that every model is partial and "represents one square in the quilt, one voice in the conversation, one angle of vision."[15] I also draw on Delwin Brown's notions of the theologian as the tradition's caretaker, one who is engaged in the "creative reconstruction of inherited symbols, the construction of a tradition's future from the resources of its past."[16] He explains this approach in the following way:

> Theology accepts as a starting point what a tradition has been and is, accepts as a goal what it might be and should become, and accepts as an obligation the advocacy of that potential realization. If a tradition is right for the time, theology will sustain and enhance it. If a tradition becomes shallow, its hidden depths will be uncovered, explored, and proclaimed. If it becomes silent, the tradition will be made to say what it can. If it feigns uniformity, the tradition's diversity, actual and potential, will be held up to view. And whenever the tradition is wrong, [theology will act to] condemn it, to challenge it, and to work for its transformation.[17]

This sort of engagement of our theological heritage, and of models of God, is not unfamiliar to feminist theologians or women in the church.[18] Long before Mary Daly's blunt observation that "If God is male, then the male is God,"[19] women (and others) have been suggesting images and metaphors for God that draw on and make sense of women's experiences. Similarly, the work of scholars such as Jean Miller Schmidt to reconstruct and reclaim women's stories within the tradition has created spaces of resonance and possibility for contemporary women.[20] It is within this same trajectory that I offer the following images and stories for God, with the hope that construction and transformation of our symbols may offer new possibilities for inclusive ecclesiology.

15. McFague, *Body of God*, viii.

16. Brown, *Boundaries*, 148.

17. Ibid.

18. I am using *feminist* here to include a broad variety of theological perspectives and critiques generated by women, rather than in the narrow meaning that focuses primarily on middle-class, educated, White women's perspectives.

19. Daly, *Beyond God the Father*, 19.

20. This sense of resonance is described more fully in Schmidt, *Grace Sufficient*, "Introduction" (particularly p. 20) and "Conclusion" (particularly p. 295).

## Assessing Existing Models of God

The process of imagining God from disability includes two elements: assessing existing images of God and proposing alternative models for God. With each step, we ask questions such as: "What does this God say about disability?" "Where does disability fit in this theology?" "What kind of meaning is attributed to disability?" "Where is disability judged, evaluated, or made invisible?" and "How does this image of God function in the real lives of people with disabilities?" This is similar in some ways to the questions of early feminist theology: if one looks at God (or church, or religious history texts, or hymnals) as a woman, or as someone concerned with women's experiences, what do you notice? As feminist theologians have shown us, one possibility is to ask whether "man" includes women. Another is to wonder what the implications are for girls who only hear stories of men in the Bible or only see men in the pulpit. Another, as Schmidt has done, is to grieve the loss of and then work to gather and reconstruct the stories of women in the tradition. And, as Schmidt's narratives portray, yet another option is to continue to claim women's authority, challenge gender disparity, and actively struggle against experiences of exclusion.

Looking at religion from the perspective of disability can lead to similarly interesting questions, as well as to similar sorts of responses or outcomes. The last twenty years have seen significant changes in the relationships between disability and religion, particularly related to access and inclusion, as a variety of factors have converged to give many churches and other religious communities the nudge they need to take seriously the presence (and, too often, the absence) of people with disabilities.[21] Yet even today people with disabilities are frequently excluded from religious services by barriers of architecture and attitude. Even when congregations have worked to make their sanctuaries accessible, it is not uncommon to find that areas such as the pulpit, altar, choir loft, or youth room still possess significant barriers. Pastors and worship leaders still perpetuate unrealistic images of people with disabilities as pitiful or inspirational, and language offensive to people with disabilities is used uncritically, leading to what Brett Webb-Mitchell calls "the betrayal of people with

21. Much of this popular momentum seems to have coincided with the passage in the United States of the Americans with Disabilities Act (ADA) of 1990. It should be noted, however, that most religious organizations were exempted from the provisions of the ADA. For more information on this historical trajectory, see Pelka, *ABC-CLIO Companion.*

disabilities."[22] While many people with disabilities have found welcome in religious communities, others still wait outside the gate.

Kathy Black, in *A Healing Homiletic*, discusses and critiques some of the traditional explanations for why a person experiences disability:

1. it is punishment for their sin or for the sin of their parents,
2. it is a test of their faith and character,
3. it is an opportunity for personal development or for the development of those in relationship to persons with disabilities,
4. it presents an opportunity for the power of God to be made manifest,
5. suffering is redemptive, and
6. the mysterious omnipotence of God simply makes it impossible to know why it is God's will.[23]

According to Black, it is a basic human desire to make sense of suffering. She notes that a common Christian explanation for any experience of suffering is that it must be God's will. But when we equate disability with suffering, we only see people with disabilities as objects to be avoided, to be admired, to be pondered, or to be pitied, rather than as full and complex human beings. While we might like to think that such blunt statements are things of the past, most people with disabilities can still tell versions of those stories. Perhaps instead of hearing about sin or saintliness, what we hear is pity or inspiration, but this sense of being "special" is still here, even if under the surface. Often, this understanding of disability as something that is "special"—a curse or a blessing, a test or a sign—has to do with default images of an omnipotent God who functions almost like a great puppeteer, controlling and determining everything, including experiences of disability. This may well be a coherent and beneficial image if applied consistently to all experiences, if both nondisability as well as disability are understood as being governed by God in this way. Yet it seems highly problematic if this image of God is only referenced to explain disability and not nondisability, particularly if such an image functions to negate agency, and deny the personhood of the person with disability.

Within traditions that do not draw on an image of an omnipotent God, a different tendency is toward a contemporary liberal answer: God

22. Webb-Mitchell, *Unexpected Guests*, 9.
23. Black, *A Healing Homiletic*, 23.

does not cause disability. Perhaps God put the laws of nature into motion and then just stepped back. Perhaps disability is just part of the way the universe works. Here one might imagine that God is with us in the experience of disability, but is "off the hook" as far as the cause is concerned. This image may function more effectively for some people than a picture of an old man in the sky who decided which people should experience life with disability. But there are also problems that come along with this claim. For example, it is not hard to see that there tends to be an implicit notion that, not only is disability something random, but that it is a random aberration, an error. It is my sense that, just as we do not accept a notion of omnipotence unevenly applied, so we should not accept a randomness response unless it is evenly applied, and we do not often hear randomness as the (theological) explanation for ability. Randomness also does not help with advocacy (it gives no motivation for people or congregations to pay attention to people with disabilities) and does not have a particularly strong pull within the Christian tradition, which tends to avoid notions of God as irrelevant to our lives, or of any aspect of our lives as irrelevant to God. Beyond this, this sort of dismissal due to randomness does not help to explain why it is, statistically at least, more "normal" to experience disability at some point in our lives rather than to be solely able bodied.

Given that neither the omnipotence model nor the randomness model seems to offer symbolic understandings for God that help us attend carefully to disability, and that neither helps us imagine new models of inclusion for our religious communities, let us turn instead to images of God that might offer different possibility spaces. Here I invite readers to creatively imagine with me what we might say about God if we take disability as something that is, relatively, normal. If we begin with the notion that people (including people with disabilities) are created in the image of God (Gen 1:27), and if this createdness (including disabilities) is good (Gen 1:31), this leads to some interesting possibilities for how we think about God and how we think about what is good. These possibilities can also lead us into new models for inclusive hospitality in our congregations and beyond.

## Limits: A New Model for God

I propose the limits model as a way to reflect on the ways in which limits appear as an unsurprising part of being human. Defining disability as the opposite of "normality" leads one to think in terms of what is not. If we begin with a person who can walk and then look at one who uses a wheelchair, what is highlighted is what the person in the wheelchair cannot do. This has been our historically conditioned response to experiences of disability, and is seen most clearly under the presuppositions of the medical model of disability, where physical bodies are compared to a medical ideal and diagnosed in terms of what is lacking. However, an alternative perspective is suggested by the limits model. Approaching our understanding of humanity from the starting point of disability gives us a more flexible and realistic (or "normal," in terms of what is actually seen across the scope of the human population) vision of human limits. Limits may then be compared and considered, but they are not seen as abhorrent or abnormal.

This sort of nonnegative attention to limits has grounding in the Christian tradition. This is a theme for many of the early Christian writers, who argued that humans are (obviously, for them) different from God and also experience a necessary and healthy dependence upon God.[24] Other early writers suggested that humans are not perfect and static but rather experience processes of change and development, as can be seen in historical variations of language, culture, and understandings of the human body, and that this is an intrinsically good aspect of creation.[25] Each of these perspectives highlights, first, that humans have limits, even if this is something that modern society seems to have forgotten. A second and related claim suggests that limits are an intrinsic aspect of human existence, part of what it means to be human. This reminds us of the writings attributed to Paul where he describes how each member of the community has a different gift, and that no one on their own but rather everyone together is what makes up the body of Christ (1 Corinthians 12). Finally, the limits perspective implies that limits are "good" or, at the very least, not evil. Christians and Jews are reminded of the first creation story, where God saw all that had been created, and said that it was very good (Gen 1:31).

In contrast to these notions, our modern perspective, captured by the familiar term limited, leads us to a deficit model of anthropology. The focus is on what we lack. When the emphasis falls on the lack of certain

---

24. Creamer, *Disability and Christian Theology*, 39–50.
25. Ibid., 49–50.

abilities, we are led to one of three questions: Why do we experience these lacks (sin)? When will we overcome these lacks (afterlife)? What is the alternative to the experience of limitation (God)? All of these questions tend to be located within an image of God as omnipotent, not completely unrelated to the puppeteer mentioned earlier. By contrast, the limits model emphasizes the good (or not-evil) created nature of humanity. It explores how limits constitute our self-understandings and our relationships with others, and leads to an ethic of how we should act as a result.

The limits model highlights that the insights that come from disability are something with which we all have experience. We learn the value of curb cuts when we use a stroller, and about the challenges of uneven sidewalks when we use crutches after a skiing accident. This model also highlights that limits go far beyond those labeled as part of the province of disability, and shows that some limits are currently viewed as more normal (I cannot fly) than others (I cannot run). The limits model challenges the deficit model, suggesting that disability is not something that exists on a negative or positive side of the balance of humanity, but rather is an intrinsic, unsurprising, and valuable element of human interpretation.

Understanding disability within the limits model highlights that all people are limited to varying degrees, and offers this perspective as a foundation for theological reflection. Limits (including experiences of disability) are understood to be unsurprising, "normal," and part of the goodness of creation. Limits are no longer something to be overcome ("fixed") in search of perfection, nor is the focus exclusively on experiences of social oppression. Rather, from the limits perspective, disability might be understood as limits that are not accommodated by the environment, and sin might now be redefined as the ways in which we both exaggerate and also deny our own limits and the limits of others. We cannot pretend that we are self-sufficient, nor should we give up and say we have no power. This means living between arrogance and despair; it also means striving for authenticity in our sense of self and our relationships with others, including our relationship with God. Rather than generating pity (from the medical model) or righteous anger (from the minority model), the limits model also leads us to generative possibilities for community, emphasizing connections and interdependence rather than competition, separation, or hyperindividuality.

Imagining God from this sort of perspective, starting with the normalcy and even goodness of limits, can be a challenge for many of us who are better acquainted with images of God that highlight power, ability, omniscience, and an overall lack of limits, and who live in a world where limits are rarely named as good. It is easy to fall into the assumptions and traps of the deficit model, equating "limits" with "limited" and thus only thinking of what is lacking or what is not. The deficit model lures us into thinking that if we suggest that God knows or experiences limits, then we are simply saying that there are things that God cannot do—a stance that in some ways might even seem to some to unmake God. My invitation here is for us to set these anxieties aside, at least for a moment, and rather to imagine what sorts of qualities an experience of limits might invite or make possible, and whether these are qualities we might also imagine (or want to imagine) for God. In other words, I invite us to consider what sorts of things limits might add, rather than just what they might take away.

## The Accessible God

A first helpful image comes from the work of Jennie Weiss Block, a disability professional with an interest in theological metaphors for disability. In the book *Copious Hosting* she proposes what she calls "a theology of access," the goal of which is to ensure "that people with disabilities take their rightful place within the Christian community."[26] This theology of access is grounded in her belief that people with disabilities are a unique group not because they are inferior to nondisabled people but rather because they are oppressed by society. Because she believes that Christian communities have an obligation to challenge oppressive structures, she calls for church communities to make changes that lead to full access and inclusion for people with disabilities.

Block sees the lens of access and inclusion as a useful one through which to examine images of God. She argues that the lens of disability highlights a God who is unfailingly committed to inclusion and access. This, she says, was the message of Jesus: all are welcome, and all have a place. According to Block, New Testament accounts show that Jesus included all people in his ministry, regardless of nationality, gender, background, or physical condition. For her, these stories of Jesus tell us what God is like, and what we are to be like as well.

Block's proposal highlights disability as an issue of oppressive structures and exclusion. Because of this, the Accessible God not only offers

26. Block, *Copious Hosting*, 11.

us images of inclusion but also calls for an end to oppressive structures. Block argues that a theology of access demands the participation of people with disabilities in decisions that affect their lives. This concrete level of inclusion is the practical goal of her theological reflections. For example, she tells of a chapel that underwent extensive remodeling to become accessible to people with disabilities, but the designers failed to consult anyone who actually uses a wheelchair—the unfortunate result being that the "accessible" chapel doesn't allow for the turn radius of a wheelchair. She uses this story to suggest that, it is not only a practical error to exclude people with disabilities from decisions that concern them, but that it is also a theological error. Those involved in making decisions about the remodeling had good intentions but were not following the gospel mandate of inclusion to its fullest extent, and were not acting in a way that is consistent with her understanding of the Accessible God. In this way, we see that the Accessible God is more than just a picture or a passive metaphor. It rather functions as a powerful symbol that demands particular responsibilities and actions by those who engage it.

## The Interdependent God

A second helpful image comes from Kathy Black, a professor of preaching who identifies herself as a person with a physical disability and who has worked for many years in Deaf ministry. In *A Healing Homiletic*, she proposes a "theology of interdependence," which emphasizes her understanding of Christian community as a place where all are called to "work interdependently with God to achieve well-being for ourselves and others."[27] Black rejects the idea of God as the great puppeteer, one who determines (or at least purposefully allows) both natural disasters and personal crises. She suggests that this conception would place God "in the position of being responsible for nuclear accidents, wars, rape, the hole in the ozone layer, homelessness, famine, toxic waste dumps, and earthquakes, as well as disability"—consequences that she finds unacceptable.[28]

Her argument is that God is not a great puppeteer, but rather that human choice is one among many factors that determine our lives. Instead of worrying too much about causes, she looks at what this means for the world around us. For Black, the stories of Jesus, especially the story

27. Black, *A Healing Homiletic*, 37–38.
28. Ibid., 34.

of the resurrection, and stories of early Christian communities, emphasize the ways in which we are all dependent upon each other, working
together to live into God's vision. God is present in the midst of life and
in the midst of suffering, offering possibilities for transformation. Thus
she takes phrases such as "the family of God," "communion of the saints,"
and "body of Christ" to directly represent people who are interdependent
upon one another and upon God, and God's interdependence with us,
not only in times of crisis but on a regular basis as well.

For Black, awareness of interdependence is a contribution that can
be made from the lens of disability. She notes that most people with
disabilities have an enhanced awareness that they are dependent upon
someone or something, whether a sign language interpreter, a guide
dog, or a wheelchair. Rather than perceiving this as a problem (which
would mean implying that people with disabilities are "dependent"), she
suggests instead that people with disabilities may be more *aware* of dependence, which in turn also allows us to also recognize that no one is
totally independent. The experience of disability allows us to see what
is often invisible to others: all people, disabled or not, are dependent on
other people and on the resources of the natural world for survival. Black
notes that this is a particularly difficult awareness within the context of
American culture, which accentuates independence and sees dependence
as something to be avoided. Black thinks that Christian communities can
offer an alternative to this standard American picture, celebrating our
interdependence. Black suggests that the Interdependent God is with us
and teaches us to be with each other, acknowledging interconnection and
valuing community, depending on each other for life.

## The Disabled God

One of the most powerful and creative images to come out of disability
theology is found in Nancy Eiesland's book titled *The Disabled God*.[29] A
person with a disability herself, Eiesland argues that traditional images
of God, especially those that lead to views of disability as either a blessing or a curse, are inadequate. Within her own experience, she wondered
whether an omnipotent God could even understand disability, let alone
be relevant in her own life. While working at a rehabilitation hospital, she
asked the residents one day what they thought.

29. Eiesland, *The Disabled God*.

"After a long silence, a young African-American man said, 'If God was in a sip-puff, maybe He would understand.' I was overwhelmed by this image: God in a sip-puff wheelchair, the kind used by many quadriplegics that enables them to maneuver the chair by blowing and sucking on a straw-like device. Not an omnipotent, self-sufficient God, but neither a pitiable, suffering servant. This was an image of God as a survivor, as one of those whom society would label 'not feasible,' 'unemployable,' with 'questionable quality of life.'"[30]

Eiesland made a connection between this image and the resurrection story in which Jesus appears to his followers and reveals his injured hands and feet (Luke 24:36–39). Eiesland suggests that Jesus reveals the Disabled God, and shows that divinity (as well as humanity) is fully compatible with experiences of disability. The *imago Dei* includes pierced hands and feet and side. According to Eiesland, this Disabled God is part of the "hidden history" of Christianity, because we rarely pay attention to the resurrected Christ as a deity whose hands, feet, and side bear the marks of profound physical impairment. As Rebecca Chopp notes in the introduction to Eiesland's work, "The most astonishing fact is, of course, that Christians do not have an able-bodied God as their primal image. Rather, the Disabled God promising grace through a broken body is at the center of piety, prayer, practice, and mission."[31]

Like Block, Eiesland finds the relevance of the Disabled God to be grounded in God's ability to be in solidarity with those who are oppressed. The image also opens the door to the theological task of rethinking Christian symbols, metaphors, rituals, and doctrines to make them accessible to people with disabilities. Eiesland's liberatory theology of disability comes from the perspective of people with disabilities and addresses people with disabilities as its central concern. For Eiesland, people who have experienced disability have an epistemological privilege: they see things that are invisible to others. As a result, any theology of disability must be done not only for, but also by, people with disabilities.

Eiesland's image of God also has specific characteristics. First, the Disabled God rejects the notion that disability is in any way a consequence of individual sin. She sees the scars of Jesus as verifying this claim: Jesus did not sin, yet became disabled. The invitation to touch Jesus' hands

---

30. Eiesland, "Encountering the Disabled God," 13.
31. Eiesland, *The Disabled God*, 11.

and side shows that taboos against disability are to be rejected, and that shallow expressions of sympathy and pity are inappropriate. She argues that God is in solidarity with people with disabilities and others who are oppressed. This is a God who has experienced and understands pain and rejection. Eiesland suggests that the Disabled God emphasizes relationality over hierarchy, values embodiment in all its diversity, and provides a profound example of inclusion, love, and acceptance—inspiring and inviting us to do the same.

These three particular images—of God who knows about access, interdependence, and disability itself—are, of course, not the only stories that come from a foundation of limits. This, too, is an insight we gain from reflection on disability, that there is an unending quantity of diversity in human life, and that we must be cautious when we note commonalities to not also overlook the beauty and complexity of radical diversity. For example, these three images draw largely on the notion of disability as an experience of social oppression and as a static condition. Other images for God might be developed to speak more clearly about what is sometimes gained from dealing with experiences of disability related to grief, loss, or impairment. These might draw on numerous biblical stories that show God as One who knows patience, sadness, or frustration. The continuum of disability (that we all have some experiences that are related to disability) and the fluidity of disability (that we may experience it in different ways at various times in our lives) can lead to images of God that emphasize creativity, a quality we see throughout Scripture and something that often arises out of experiences of limits. Finally, we must remember that limits are not only experienced by people with disabilities, but by all of us. That we all experience limits, and that we were created as good in the image of God, might itself remind us of a God whose values, goals, and criteria for evaluation might be very different than our own, a God of Love beyond our understanding.

## Toward Inclusive Ecclesiology and Genuine Hospitality

Models of God that begin with the embrace of limits offer powerful alternatives to traditional images. They demonstrate that the idea of God is not incompatible with disability, and, moreover, that it is possible to argue that God is for or on the side of people with disabilities. Such models help explain to churches why they must attend to issues of justice, sending clear and unequivocal messages about the intrinsic value of people with disabilities. We are not a problem; we are of God. You do not include me as a favor to me, but rather because I am part of the goodness of creation. The memorable image of the Disabled God, as One who intimately knows and even experiences disability, is especially important: in addition to calling for change, it irrevocably changes the way one encounters the Christian story. How can one be a Christian and not value experiences of disability? The image necessarily leads to changes in understanding and in action. The models discussed above do just that: offer new paths and new possibilities for inclusive ecclesiology. They show us that accessibility is about more than just ramps and updated hymns and special services; the question of accessibility matters all the way through to the very core of our community practices as well as our belief systems.

Disability theology allows us to go beyond issues of accessibility, offering new images, understandings, and practices that draw on the knowledge and insights that come from the vast and diverse experiences of disability and human limits. These insights are helpful not just to people with disabilities, or to families and others who care about people with disabilities, but to all of us as we go about the task of creating inclusive communities that model genuine hospitality—places where all truly are welcome. We are challenged by these God-images to include the other, not because doing so is politically correct, and not because we feel guilty if we do not, but rather because we learn to recognize the intrinsic value and the presence of God in each other, and even in ourselves.

As with other theological tasks, the work ahead is more than simply changing the words we use or the pictures we imagine when we think about God or about church. None of these models is sufficient alone; each has dangers and each has limits. We are reminded that the God who is beyond all understanding cannot be captured in a single image or metaphor, and so our tendency to rely primarily or exclusively on a particular image will lead us away from the richness of other possibilities of knowing or being. Drawing on this sense of the diversity of experiences we each have, in our bodies and beyond, this focus on inclusive ecclesiology becomes an invitation for each of us to share and describe and play with our own "lenses," to reflect on how we each touch and feel and move through this world. Inclusive ecclesiology invites you to share these stories and to listen with care to each other's stories as we work to build communities and congregations that are open to the sacred and welcoming to all.

# BIBLIOGRAPHY

Black, Kathy. *A Healing Homiletic: Preaching and Disability.* Nashville: Abingdon, 1996.

Block, Jennie Weiss. *Copious Hosting: A Theology of Access for People with Disabilities.* New York: Continuum, 2002.

Brown, Delwin. *Boundaries of Our Habitations: Traditions and Theological Construction.* Albany: State University of New York Press, 1994.

Creamer, Deborah Beth. *Disability and Christian Theology: Embodied Limits and Constructive Possibilities.* Oxford: Oxford University Press, 2009.

Daly, Mary. *Beyond God the Father: Toward a Philosophy of Women's Liberation.* Boston: Beacon Press, 1973.

Eiesland, Nancy. *The Disabled God: Toward a Liberatory Theology of Disability.* Nashville: Abingdon, 1994.

————. "Encountering the Disabled God." *The Other Side* 38/5 (2002) 10–15.

Harris Interactive. "Kessler Foundation/National Organization on Disability 2010 Survey of People with Disabilities." Online: http://www.2010disabilitysurveys.org/.

McFague, Sallie. *The Body of God: An Ecological Theology.* Minneapolis: Fortress, 1993.

————. "An Earthly Theological Agenda." *Christian Century* 108 (1991) 12–15.

Musser, Donald W., and Joseph L. Price, editors. *A New Handbook of Christian Theology.* Nashville: Abingdon, 1992.

Pelka, Fred. *The ABC-CLIO Companion to the Disability Rights Movement.* ABC-CLIO Companions to Key Issues in American History and Life. Santa Barbara: ABC-CLIO, 1997.

Russell, Letty R. *Church in the Round: Feminist Interpretation of the Church.* Louisville: Westminster John Knox, 1993.

Russell, Letty R., and J. Shannon Clarkson, editors. *Dictionary of Feminist Theologies.* Louisville: Westminster John Knox, 1996.

Schmidt, Jean Miller. *Grace Sufficient: A History of Women in American Methodism, 1760–1939.* Nashville: Abingdon, 1999.

Thislethwaite, Susan Brooks, and Mary Potter Engel, editors. *Lift Every Voice: Constructing Christian Theologies from the Underside.* Revised and expanded ed. Maryknoll: Orbis, 1998.

United States Census Bureau. *Americans with Disabilities: 2005.* Online: http://www.census.gov/prod/2008pubs/p70-117.pdf/.

Webb-Mitchell, Brett. *Unexpected Guests at God's Banquet: Welcoming People with Disabilities into the Church.* New York: Crossroad, 1994. Reprinted, Eugene, OR: Wipf & Stock, 2009.

# Pastoral Response

## James Burns

ONE DAY, WHILE WALKING along a quiet street in Philadelphia, I happened upon a lovely old church. It had a well-worn sign out front, and something caught my eye that didn't seem quite right. On the bottom of the sign, where I expected to see the words "Visitors Welcome," there was this wording instead: "Visitors Expected."

That gives a different message! Not a passive stance that suggests "we will scoot over and make a little room for outsiders" but a promise that proclaims "we have thought through, prayed about, and made the changes necessary for new kinds of people to truly belong." Deborah Creamer begins her chapter on how churches may best extend hospitality to people of all abilities with a reflection on welcome. She spends little time addressing problems with physical building space in favor of speaking to barriers of attitude. This is not because architectural redesign is unimportant. But in some ways fixing that is the easy part. True hospitality requires changes in the theological understanding of the people as well.

I write this response as a pastor who has served Metropolitan Community Churches (primarily serving the lesbian and gay community) in New Haven, Houston, and Denver. This means that I have shared the same struggles to be genuinely welcoming of people with disabilities as any pastor would. It also means that I bring the experience of another commonly excluded group to the discussion: sexual minorities. We too know the difference between being welcomed in name and in fact. For example, Creamer cites the United Methodist slogan "Open Hearts, Open Minds, Open Doors." Those of us who find our most profound relationships, and

45

our most sincere calls to ordination, denied by that church have the right to wonder how truly "open" they are, and how truly "welcome" we are.

Creamer begins by describing the continuum of disability. None of us is either able or disabled but instead fall on a range, which also changes over time (fluidity). This insight may be expanded to recognize that there are in fact multiple continuums; a person who cannot walk may have better hearing than another who can. It may help to imagine a three-dimensional scale, with lines branching in all directions.

This is helpful in understanding all manner of differences. We human beings are fond of thinking in polarities: people are either able or disabled, black or white, male or female, gay or straight, conservative or liberal, rich or poor. But none of these categorizations are as simple as they sound. Most people's ethnic heritages are far more complicated than a two-ended scale can account for, and our sexualities are probably as unique as our fingerprints. The better we understand exactly who we are and who our neighbor is, the less likely we are to fall into the trap of "us versus them," and the more likely we are to notice our similarities alongside our differences.

This leads to Creamer's core concept: the limits model. All of us can do some things well, none of us can do everything well, and this is a key to understanding the nature of creation and of God. One implication of this insight for churches is that we cannot, and need not try to, reach every person in the same way through everything we do.

For example, our church has become very practiced in the art of using visual images on screen to enhance preaching. For the past four years I have taught a session of Eunjoo Kim's Introduction to Christian Worship class at Iliff School of Theology. As I describe what we have learned about the power of images, someone will usually ask about visually impaired people in the congregation. Shouldn't we avoid using visual resources that not everyone will be able to appreciate?

Creamer's limits model helps to explain why the answer is no. While we should make every effort to accommodate as much as we can, we will never reach the place where every part of the service is equally accessible. We sing hymns and hear anthems, even though they cannot be fully appreciated by all (even with ASL interpretation). We speak sermons, although some are not auditory learners. We perform rituals, despite the fact that not everyone has a spiritual type that finds them meaningful. The very elements that one group finds difficult to respond to may be especially meaningful to other people, and vice versa. A responsibly planned service will attend to the widest possible range of potential worshippers, while acknowledging that everyone will access some parts more easily than others.

What our world calls weaknesses may be re-imagined as strengths. Creamer wonders "what it would look like to consider disability as a normal experience and even as part of the goodness of creation."[1] I vividly remember a short documentary I watched in college about a woman who had been born with only one limb. When asked how she felt about herself, she replied, "I think I am perfect." I recall how surprised I was to hear this.

I would be less surprised now, thanks to role models I have had in my life. It made a difference that my preaching professor at Yale Divinity School, Lee McGee, is legally blind. When we feature readers at our service who have a speech impediment or walk with a cane, it illustrates what a range of humanity God has created. How much would we benefit from hearing preachers with disabilities? What insights on the Bible's healing stories might they offer?

I once heard Barbara Lundblad, preaching professor at Union Seminary, lament, "Where are the healing stories in the Bible that don't end in a cure?" Many of us make a distinction between cure and healing, using *cure* to refer to the ending of a physical malady, and *healing* to describe a spiritual experience of attaining God's peace, with or without a cure. Her question made me think of a midrash I had written, a first-person narrative from the perspective of the hemorrhaging woman who touched Jesus's garment. It begins with her saying,

> *I have a secret.*
> *My secret is . . . I bleed. Every day. Just a little.*
> *Not enough that it interferes with my daily activities.*
> *A nuisance, nothing more. It would be a minor inconvenience,*
> *except . . .*
> *Except for the Law.*
> *You know the Law. It says that when a woman bleeds,*
> *she is unclean. And anything and anyone she touches*
> *becomes unclean. Untouchable. Invisible to God.*
> *Can you even imagine what it's like, every night, asking*
> *God why I was made this way, begging God to take it away?*
> *Every morning I would eagerly look down at my sheets,*
> *hoping against hope that they would be clean. But they*
> *never were. I always saw blood.*

1. See p. 28 above.

The midrash continues as she seeks out and encounters Jesus. It concludes with Jesus saying:

> *"Daughter, don't you know, you are whole,*
> *you are blessed, you are healed, your faith has made it so.*
> *Let the Law trouble you no more."*
> *I know what you are wondering. Do I still bleed?*
> *Every day, just a little. Oh I know the disciples started*
> *a rumor "And immediately the flow of blood stopped."*
> *They didn't ask me. They still tell that story, and I still*
> *bleed. But I am healed, that's what the rabbi taught me,*
> *and I don't let the Law trouble me any longer.*
> *I touch whomever I want, without fear.*
> *And every morning, when I look down at the sheets and*
> *see blood, I give thanks. I give thanks.*

I wrote this as a metaphor for the experience of queer people, who often are taught we need to reject a part of ourselves. But with grace we experience healing that convinces us that no change is required. Similarly, with respect to people with disabilities, it is the church that is required to change its attitudes. A full spectrum of abilities is created by God, called good, and used for God's purpose. Creamer's chapter helps us to imagine a church that empowers everyone to give thanks for who they are, a church that is truly welcoming to all.

# Chapter Three

## Holy Spirit, Communities of Faith, and Leadership

### Catherine L. Kelsey

RAPID CHANGE IS A regular feature of North American culture in the twenty-first century. The stress of it is felt in many kinds of organizations, as well as by individuals. One of the common responses in historic Christian organizations has been a proliferation of conversations about leadership: "If only clergy leaders would do this . . .", "If at least some lay leaders would do that . . ." A few of these conversations have been about cultivating leadership skills of one particular kind or another.[1] Considerable borrowing from studies of business leadership occurs in these conversations. The goal is to foster the kind of responsiveness in Christian organizations that cultural change seems to require.

I propose to initiate an additional conversational thread about leadership here. I invite readers to engage in theological reflection on how divine presence is manifest in the world, in order to see what light it might shed on distinctively Christian foundations for leadership. In a nutshell: The theological purpose of Christian communities of faith is to

---

1. See, for instance, the work of Roxburgh and Romanuk on "missional leadership" in *The Missional Leader*.

cooperate with the *missio Dei*, what God is doing in the world expressly through Holy Spirit.[2] To the extent that this theological purpose is actually the purpose-in-practice, leadership of communities of faith has the aim of facilitating the discernment and responsiveness of the community to what Holy Spirit is doing in the community's location. This is a particular role for leadership, unparalleled in organizations defined by human purposes alone.

In my experience as a clergy leader, women tend to be more aware than men of two features of human life that deeply influence leadership, namely: 1) each human being is irreplaceable without damage to other persons; and 2) our influence lies in the quality of our relationships. These two insights may arise in multiple ways in women's lives, but they are especially clear in the relationship between mother and child.[3] Mothering and the roles of mothering can be expressed by women, or by men, who are not a child's biological mother. Yet, there appears to be a wound, not a fatal one but a wound nevertheless, when the relationship between biological mother and child is absent. Persons are not interchangeable, we are not simply a collection of roles that anyone could play. Rather, we experience these roles and the bonds of relationship differently with different persons. Each person is unique and therefore each relationship is unique and irreplaceable. Mothering is one of many kinds of common experiences among women that lead women to attend to the particularity of relationships. Consequently, women are frequently attentive to leadership practices that acknowledge the individuality of each relationship between leader and those with whom she works, either collectively or individually.

My account of how Holy Spirit is manifest in the particularity of relationships is not limited to women's leadership. But perhaps it can be articulated first by a woman because, like many other women, I am especially attentive to the particularity of relationships. In this chapter I direct

2. Framing the purpose of Christian communities in this way is significantly influenced by the conversation about mission initiated by David Bosch's work, *Transforming Mission*. Seeing organizational purpose as cooperation with God's activity immediately moves beyond human needs and purposes alone. I grant that divine purpose cannot be fully known within the human realm; the invitation here is to use the full extent of what Christians do understand of divine purposes—*missio Dei*—to theorize leadership within Christian communities of faith and the particular practices of leadership that Christian leaders might contribute to civic community.

3. I am not making an essentialist argument here. In white, middle-class American culture in the later twentieth and early twenty-first centuries, this is the way I have observed women relate to their own biological mothers, adoptive mothers, and mentors.

the reader's attention to the particularity of Christian relationship with Holy Spirit.[4] Leaders do not act in precisely the same way that Holy Spirit acts, but I propose that those who lead effectively in communities of faith anticipate the ways in which Holy Spirit engages relationally. Leaders help the entire faith community receive and respond to the ways God chooses to be in relationship.

The description of Holy Spirit's engagement which I offer here will move in three steps. I begin with the relationship between Holy Spirit and individuals as it is complexly theorized by John Wesley, whose theological influence in American religious thought extends beyond the various branches of Methodism into holiness movements, evangelical movements, and Pentecostal movements. Second, the complexity of individual experience of Holy Sprit invites an equally complex theorization of Holy Spirit in communities of faith, which thus leads here beyond Wesley to the thought of Friedrich Schleiermacher. Then, third, leadership in those communities of faith will be theorized here based on my own observation. This three-step theory, in turn, suggests a provocative conclusion about the qualities necessary for both lay and clergy who are designated as leaders in faith community.

## The Work of Holy Spirit in Individuals

John Wesley's theology of Holy Spirit's work of redemption and sanctification in individuals contributed to the liberation of persons whose individual worth was not thoroughly affirmed in their cultural context. [5] In both England and North America, the appeal of Wesleyan theological emphases, particularly universal atonement, was that those emphases were perceived as undermining existing structures that privileged persons with more economic means. That is, all persons are seen to be

4. I choose not to use a definite article with "Holy Spirit" as a means of destabilizing the tendency to objectify the subjectivity of a reality with whom we constantly interact. Without the definite article, "Holy Spirit" functions more like a personal name, one with whom we are in relationship as we speak the name.

5. I am glad to have an opportunity to acknowledge my indebtedness to Jean Miller Schmidt's historical work. Her interrogation of the relationship between cultures and the faith experience of marginalized persons, particularly women, invites some of the questions for our own constructive theological thinking that this chapter seeks to explore. Without the recognition of those relationships in Methodism's past, it is almost impossible to explore them in the present. Her students and readers continue to experience the challenge to engage in liberating praxis that her work invites.

recipients of divine grace, and all persons who respond to that grace with trust and the will to grow in holiness with divine help are honored in the faith community. Economic means is neither an indicator of one's status with God nor a source of privilege; rather, economic means yields both greater responsibility and the threat of greater temptation.

Following Albert Outler's interpretive direction, we can identify two primary ways in which John Wesley theorized the Christian community's experience of Holy Spirit as a distinctive expression of the triune God.[6] First, Wesley held that Holy Spirit is the source of life itself, both for all creatures and, further, in a distinctive way, for human beings, made in a certain likeness to the divine.[7] The metaphor of breath and of spirit as breath operates as a description of dependence on the divine power which inspires life in all its forms, moment by moment, breath by breath. Human being then also receives its distinctive identity thereby, a likeness to God that is sustained immediately by Holy Spirit.

The second theorization is at the core of Wesley's preaching to evangelize and elicit response: Holy Spirit is witness to our individual adoption as children of God.[8] This witness has two acts, each of which is gifted by the Spirit, an internal witness and our own spirit's response. The internal witness may or may not have a voice. It consists in a personal appropriation of God's justifying act in Jesus Christ—in particular, knowing that Christ died, not just for the world, but also *for me*. Such knowledge is not merely intellectual or theoretical, it is personal in a way that provides complete assurance of one's own status in relationship with God. *I* am assuredly beloved and redeemed. Such a conviction comes as a gift rather than as an achievement. It is deemed, without doubt, to be a direct work of the Spirit.

This internal witness is seconded by the witness of our own spirits in response. Our spirits produce fruits—inward fruits of joy, peace, and holiness of mind and outward fruits of love-of-neighbor and holiness-of-action.[9] These fruits also come to us as gifts, gifts with which we choose to cooperate. Because we are aware that we were not capable on our own of generating the fruits, it is clear to us that they, too, are gifts of the Spirit.

6. Outler, "A Focus on the Holy Spirit," 3–18.

7. Wesley, "Sermon 118," II.1, 42; "Sermon 117," §7, 32; "Sermon 120," §21, 69.

8. Wesley, "Sermon 10," I.10, 275.

9. Wesley, "Sermon 10," I.11, 275–76.

It might seem possible either to falsely identify the internal witness or to mimic the fruits. We could get caught up in an emotional moment and convince ourselves that we are assured, or we could produce the evidence of fruits as an act of will, making the fruits into our own works.[10] In Wesley's mind, there is no doubt about the divine source when *both* have appeared. The presence of Holy Spirit is then unmistakable.

In arriving at that twofold account, Wesley assumes five features in his references to Holy Spirit. First, this Spirit has agency. It can and does act independently in and through the world and the world's constituent parts, human and nonhuman. Second, Holy Spirit works in individual lives in direct and immediate ways. Third, on principle, there is no reason that Spirit cannot work in every single individual—it does not respect rank or human forms of privilege. Fourth, what can limit the work of Holy Spirit is an individual's negative exercise of free will. Holy Spirit requires cooperation—at a minimum, passive cooperation. Holy Spirit respects individual free will. This assumption is a necessary correlate of human responsibility. If the Spirit could override free will, then any person whose will the Spirit chooses not to override would no longer be responsible for the consequences of one's exercise of that free will. Fifth, Holy Spirit is focused on individual transformation. The reign of God over civic structures and communities is not addressed. It is the case that inward individual holiness is expected to result in relational, social holiness between persons. But the social structures that love requires are not a focus of Spirit's direct attention—not, at least, in Wesley's preached account of Spirit. This lacuna does not mean that some of these structures are beyond Wesley's attention in practice. Rather, it indicates that the practices are not theorized as work of Holy Spirit in his preaching.

Wesley did attend carefully to the creation of communities of accountability in the creation of class meeting—the fundamental unit of the Methodist Societies in the eighteenth century and in the first third of the nineteenth century. One was a member of a class meeting, not of a church or of a worshipping community. Participation in a class meeting was the necessary prerequisite for participation in the sacramental worship life of the Societies, particularly love feasts at quarterly conference.[11] The practice of class meeting included several practices of community that might

10. Wesley, "Sermon 10," deals with these issues explicitly, as does "Sermon 11," V.3–4, 297–98.

11. Richey et al., *The Methodist Experience*, 1:96–97.

be theorized as work of Holy Spirit. In particular, confession, forgiveness, and discernment (including both problem solving and identifying goals and decision making), each of which occurs with greater power in the context of a gathering of two or more. When these elements are theorized in light of Wesley's theorization of each individual's responsibility, they are transformed from mechanisms for control of a class of people to mechanisms of their own empowerment. And that appears to be how they were experienced and why they were embraced by many early participants in the Methodist movement.[12]

Wesley's theorization of individual responsibility for responding to God, not just initially at justification but continually through sanctification, yielded an anthropology in which every person is recognized as responsible. Responsibility is possible only when an individual's free will is recognized as a constituent feature of his or her personhood. Every individual's agency was supposed to be recognized, affirmed, and strengthened by the practices of the movement. In the cultural context of eighteenth century England and its colonies, this combination was revolutionary. It appealed particularly to women, to slaves and free Blacks, and to white men whose skills as artisans were potentially skills as small entrepreneurs.[13]

Wesley himself did not exist within these classes of persons. As a consequence, he did not seem to fully grasp or appreciate the power of the transformation in identity involved. This factor is clearly visible in his attempts to maintain control over the movement of Methodists in North America—control that made sense for him to hold from the perspective of the old social order and that made no sense at all to those in North America who had experienced freedom and responsibility in Christ through the direct work of Holy Spirit.

Wesley's theorization of Holy Spirit arrives at its limit as we turn from considering Spirit's work in individual lives to considering Spirit's work in communities of faith.

---

12. The response of women and of both enslaved and free Africans in America impelled the movement, as testified by membership records and the oft-repeated founding stories about Barbara Heck, Elizabeth Strawbridge and others. See ibid., 1:54–58, 100–101; and Schmidt, *Grace Sufficient*.

13. See the opening chapters of Wigger, *American Saint*, for an extended historical explication of this point.

## Work of Holy Spirit in Communities of Faith

All of this focus on individual transformation as a transformation of the social order was fitted to the social situations regnant in eighteenth and nineteenth centuries. We have come to a time in North America, however, in which an individualism that was initially experienced in the context of community has come to overwhelm that very communal context. Further, by the late twentieth century individualism has been co-opted by consumerism, which simultaneously relies upon a high degree of individual choice and a low recognition of interconnectedness and mutual responsibility. This new phenomenon has given rise to the manipulation of individual desire through advertising in ways that can be experienced, in turn, as bondage—a narrowing of the capacity to recognize many of the responses available to participants within a dynamic, interconnected, living creation.

The community of faith's interaction with Holy Spirit needs to be theorized in order to temper the effects of our current cultural context. Friedrich Schleiermacher's thought demonstrates that it is possible to theorize the work of Holy Spirit in community without rejecting or obscuring the kinds of insights that Wesley articulated about the work of Holy Spirit in individuals. Schleiermacher's understanding of the work of Holy Spirit in individuals is consistent with Wesley's, but it also further articulates how individuals are interconnected into faith community as an activity of Holy Spirit's engagement.

It is not necessary to adopt Schleiermacher's specific doctrinal formulations in order to be assisted by his work. For our purposes here, we need only to identify the experiences of faith community that he seeks to explain. In *Christian Faith,* and consistently in his preaching,[14] Schleiermacher distinguished between the structures of church as institution and as a human entity, on the one hand, and the experience of faith community, on the other hand. This is completely consistent with Wesley's relationship with the Church of England, which he never left. Schleiermacher suggested that Christian communities of faith exist only within the larger context of institutional church structures, but that they are a subset of the larger context, not to be confused with the structures

14. See Kelsey, *Schleiermacher's Preaching,* for a full description of Schleiermacher's preaching and its relationships to his systematic theological work.

themselves.[15] Identifying that feature of our experience of faith community enables us to notice its existence in time as a function of the qualities of the relationships that are occurring.

Schleiermacher theorized the interpersonal context of redemption because he noticed that saving faith is closely associated with a person's being in relationship with a person of vital faith, the same kind of relationship that Jesus Christ had with each of the men and women who followed him on a daily basis.[16] For this reason, interpersonal contexts, such as the class meetings that Wesley so skillfully used as the basis of Methodist Societies, seem to be essential for the sharing of saving faith in Jesus Christ. Interpersonal contexts are a visible realm within which Holy Spirit moves and works.

This insight led Schleiermacher to attend in detail to the nature of the interpersonal contexts that constitute "church." Church is a human construction, with all of the possibilities that humans can create and all the limitations that are inevitable. Because it is a human construction, it can appropriately take many different forms, as is demonstrated in the many branches of the Christian church.[17] The form of the human construction is not its essential feature, nor what makes it "church." God's act through Holy Spirit constituting a community of faith within the human construction is what makes it church.[18] When and where there is a community of faith, that community is called into being by Holy Spirit and this Spirit is the "common spirit" of that community. The common spirit is a gift to the community in the midst of its complex relationships and interactions; it is neither an accomplishment of the community's doing nor a characteristic of the community's being apart from the gift of the Spirit in each moment.[19] A community of faith exists only by virtue of its receiving this gift as that which shapes and enlivens its human interactions

15. Schleiermacher, *Christian Faith* (1830–31), §148 and §149 on the visible and invisible church. Page numbers vary between the English translations and the available German texts. The entire group of propositions and explanatory sections named in this and further notes are the most substantial source in each instance. Because the entire work is systematic, interconnected, and thus somewhat reiterative, the propositions named provide entry points for the concept in the context of the work's full exposition.

16. Ibid., §113.1, §128.1, §100.1 all make this point. The entire account of redemption is found in §§86–105, though its implications involve the full work.

17. Ibid., §§148–52.

18. Ibid., §§121–25 on Holy Spirit as it constitutes the common spirit of the church.

19. Ibid., §116.3 and §§121–25.

within each present occasion. A community of faith is not an entity with a life of its own; rather, it exists as a gift of the Spirit. In Schleiermacher's construction, community with one another enacts communion with God in Christ. It is thereby, and at the same time, participation in the being of God, participation in divine love.[20]

Hence, a community of faith is constituted first by God's act and second by cooperation with that act—exactly the same sequence that Wesley describes in the process of individual salvation. Moreover, exactly as for individual salvation in Wesley's thought, this reception and cooperation happens moment by moment, rather than permanently in one action. Human cooperation with the gift of Spirit's constituting a community has a beginning point, to which the community will need to return again and again when the patterns of sin close it to the gift of Spirit. Patterns of sin are brought to the community by its members, can overwhelm the community from sources within its broader cultural context, and result from the community's own past habits.[21] Prior to the completion of the reign of God this rhythm of movement-into-sin and the gift of return-to-relationship are to be expected. Wesley's practices of accountability, not just for individuals but also for class meetings and societies, indicate that he shared this expectation with Schleiermacher.

Thus, Schleiermacher's theorization helps us to recognize a potential extension of Wesley's understanding of the work of Holy Spirit. A gathering in the life of a church can become a community of faith when the gathering receives and responds to a gift of Holy Spirit. The Spirit's gifts are transformative of communities, not just of individuals. This description of the work of Holy Spirit invites closer consideration of what happens within inspired communities of faith, including how leadership occurs.

## Leadership within Communities of Faith

When we theorize the activity of Holy Spirit in both individual lives and in communities of faith, specific implications begin to emerge. Here I stand on the shoulders of Wesley and Schleiermacher and also reach beyond them. Let us begin by inquiring further into the life of a community of faith itself, namely, when a community of faith is Spirit inspired, how is it functioning? Who is leading and what are they doing that leads?

20. Ibid., §166.1.
21. Ibid., §126.1.

We have already noticed that Schleiermacher's account of communities of faith parallels Wesley's account of individual faith—Spirit provides gifts and the community or particular individuals receive and cooperate with those gifts. There is joy in the receiving and eagerness to cooperate. Communities involve complex interactions between all the individual participants. What is predominantly going on when those interactions are joyfully receiving gifts from Holy Spirit? I observe that there are always kinds of listening happening, in multiple directions—kinds of listening that are all attentive and intentional and skilled. There is listening to ideas and also significant listening to emotions, some of which are too deep for words and may be uttered in ecstasy or in tears. What is heard is mirrored back to check for accuracy and to slow down the process so that it can be considered well before a response arises. This process of consideration includes comparing what is heard with other sources, pondering it for its implications, seeking out its unspoken corollaries—in a word, discernment.[22] A community of faith receives Holy Spirit's gifts through the quality of its listening together. And when complex listening, discernment, is happening in a community of faith, leadership is exercised by anyone and everyone who assists others skillfully to engage. Thus, leadership comes to be diffused throughout the community.

Within an inspired community, who seems to exercise such leadership most easily and most frequently and unobtrusively? I observe leaders who practice habits of complex listening daily—in prayer, in pondering Scripture, in holding others in the divine presence, in centering oneself on Christ's divine love as a balance point. They are practicing in their individual lives the skills of a discerning listening to Spirit as it is embodied in the biblical text, in themselves, and in the world around them. As a result of their prayer, they are familiar with a multitude of distractions to careful listening and they have identified a number of effective ways to focus on the nuances of interaction with Holy Spirit in the midst of distraction. They are aware of distortions that their lives create in their own hearing, and so they welcome comparing and sharing in the listening process with others. They are at ease in realizing the paradox that discernment simultaneously involves simplicity and complexity because they have experienced it frequently.

---

22. The word *discernment* is often associated with quiet reception. Here I intend to indicate that it may also refer to active listening and noisy responses.

Among those who are praying daily, I observe those who also seek and build significant relationships with persons who are different from themselves are those most likely to facilitate the participation of others in a community. Just as with prayer, it takes practice to become interconnected. Those who have practiced moving through the initial awkwardness of not even knowing what questions to ask as one seeks to listen, eventually come to move through the awkwardness more easily. This attitude, in turn, is represented in the hospitality of welcoming each stranger into one's life as part of the present, communal incarnation of Christ, as one who mediates divine presence in ways one has perhaps not yet more than begun to discover.

When a community of faith is Holy Spirit–inspired, persons who listen in prayer regularly and who welcome the stranger are likely to be leaders themselves, and they are likely to be able to facilitate the leadership of those who have less experience or skill. Discerning listening happens because they are helping it happen in response to and as an active presence of Holy Spirit.

Leadership in a community of faith, then, is fostered by encouraging each individual to cultivate those two aspects of their individual life—daily listening prayer and seeking connection with those who are different. Since community of faith is defined by its responsiveness to the activity of Holy Spirit, we can identify at least these two foundational practices of leadership that emerge in that condition of responsiveness.

Whether a leader is a volunteer designated for a particular role or a person whose career is set aside for leadership in church, the foundational practices for leadership when a community of faith is responsive to Holy Spirit are the same: daily listening prayer and seeking connection with those who are different. The differences between laity and clergy, between volunteer and staff, between credentials and experience, are all irrelevant at this point. When a community of faith is inspired by Holy Spirit the persons who act as leaders, fostering the participation and responsiveness of all, are practiced listeners to Holy Spirit and to persons who are quite different from them.

This tells us something significant about designated leadership as a role and skill set. Designated leaders prepare the people to exercise leadership themselves in their responses to what is gifted by Holy Spirit's presence in the community. *Designated leaders prepare environments in which a gathered people may easily and confidently receive Holy Spirit's presence and cooperate with it.* This is as true for occasions for worship, service, or learning as it is for decision-making meetings. The skills involved are not difficult to learn if and only if one is engaging in the foundational practices. Without the foundational practices there can be little recognition of the actual process of engagement with Holy Spirit as a possibility, let alone as a possibility for which preparation can be made.

Consequently, *it makes little sense to select persons as designated leaders who are not engaging in the foundational practices.* Such persons are ill equipped to assist the community to become a community of faith.[23]

## Conclusion

I have suggested here that, especially today, when old structures of functioning as individuals and as groups are rapidly changing and becoming more diverse, it would help us to recall that we are surrounded by divine presence and purpose as we are facing these changes. I have proposed that our most effective responses to change will be those that open us to Holy Spirit's presence and that help us to respond to Holy Spirit's gifts. I have also sought to indicate that leadership that is reflectively attentive to the unique qualities of each individual and each group relationship encountered could be undertaken by either a woman or a man. However, for a variety of reasons women might well find it to be a particularly attractive mode of leadership.

Viewed in general, leadership can either help or prevent individual and group responsiveness to divine presence and activity. As we have seen here, leadership informed by John Wesley would anticipate Holy Spirit's transformative work in individual lives. It would invite attention to the witness of human spirit in response to Holy Spirit and attention to evidence of fruits alongside that witness. In this approach, the result of individual interaction with Holy Spirit itself would make clear that individual responsibility is integral to human agency, experienced as true freedom. In this mode, responsible leaders, therefore, would help individuals recognize, receive, and faithfully respond to the transformative work of Holy Spirit in their lives.

In taking a further step forward, we have seen that leadership informed by Friedrich Schleiermacher, in turn, would recognize that the

---

23. I leave to a future article questions about the transferability of leadership skills from faith communities to the civic sphere.

visible work of Holy Spirit occurs through interpersonal contexts. Within these contexts, Holy Spirit would be invited and grasped in ways that enable Holy Spirit to become the common spirit, or shared spirit, among persons interacting with one another. Such leadership would demonstrate understanding of the interconnection that enlivens human encounter. Regardless of the details of how or for what purpose they are constituted, genuine communities of faith would be recognized to exist only in this particular kind of encounter shaped by Holy Spirit.

Leadership that facilitates the work of Holy Spirit within a gathered people has indeed been known to create an environment in which the people present may confidently receive Holy Spirit's presence and cooperate with it. Thus, a major question raised here is: What kind of leaders most easily create these environments? One answer advanced here is: They are persons who are practiced in listening modes of prayer and in then learning to listen deeply to persons whose life experience is very different from their own.

Of course, leadership has always involved listening in some fashion. When living in the midst of both inner and outer change, a leader's cooperating with Holy Spirit involves listening with even greater care, particularly with persons whose experience and being in the world might serve to stretch our own vision and imagination. We would not be listening for a single voice to lay out a specific way forward, as with a map. Rather, we would be listening for the harmonics and dissonances that arise between us. Holy Spirit gifts us with this music and leads us through our singing, listening, and responding together.

Leadership, as described in this chapter, is meant to help a people become a genuine community of faith as it joins and creates music with Holy Spirit in its time and location. It cooperates with the ways that some strands of Christian theology that are likewise sensitive to Holy Spirit's presence describe God's activity as present among us.

## BIBLIOGRAPHY

Bosch, David. *Transforming Mission: Paradigm Shifts in Theology of Mission.* Maryknoll, NY: Orbis, 1991.

Kelsey, Catherine L. *Schleiermacher's Preaching, Dogmatics, and Biblical Criticism: The Interpretation of Jesus Christ in the Gospel of John.* Princeton Theological Monograph Series 68. Eugene, OR: Pickwick Publications, 2007.

Outler, Albert C. "A Focus on the Holy Spirit: Spirit and Spirituality in John Wesley." *Quarterly Review* (1988) 3–18.

Richey, Russell et al. *The Methodist Experience in America.* Vol. 1, *A History.* 2 vols. Nashville: Abingdon, 2010.

Roxburgh, Alan, and Fred Romanuk. *The Missional Leader: Equipping Your Church to Reach a Changing World.* San Francisco: Jossey-Bass, 2006.

Schleiermacher, Friedrich. *Christian Faith.* 2nd, 1830–31 ed. Translated by Terrence N. Tice, Catherine L. Kelsey, and Edwina Lawler. Louisville: Westminster John Knox, forthcoming.

Schleiermacher, Friedrich. *Der christliche Glaube.* Edited by Martin Redeker. 7th ed. Berlin: de Gruyter, 1960.

Schmidt, Jean Miller. *Grace Sufficient: A History of Women in American Methodism, 1760–1939.* Nashville: Abingdon, 1999.

Wesley, John. *The Works of John Wesley.* Vol. 1, *Sermons, I, 1–33.* Edited by Albert C. Outler. Bicentennial ed. Nashville: Abingdon, 1984.

———. *The Works of John Wesley.* Vol. 4, *Sermons, IV, 115–151.* Edited by Albert C. Outler. Bicentennial ed. Nashville: Abingdon, 1987.

Wigger, John. *American Saint: Francis Asbury and the Methodists.* Oxford: Oxford University Press, 2009.

# Pastoral Response

## Eric Smith

### Leadership as Active Cooperation with the Holy Spirit

MY SPIRIT RESONATES AFFIRMATIVELY with Kelsey's discussion of the Holy Spirit's role in Christian communities of faith and leadership. In particular, I agree with her assertion that Christian leadership should actively cooperate with the *missio Dei*, what God is doing in the world through the Holy Spirit. This is a call back to our Wesleyan roots, the roots that make us distinctly Methodist.

In my twenty-five years as a United Methodist minister, I have watched with dismay as the United Methodist Church has floundered in the waves of rapid social and technological changes. In the face of monumental change we have sought to overcome the creeping crisis of irrelevance. That is to say, we have tried to remain relevant to the people who have grown up in the twentieth century while learning to be relevant to young people who are comfortable with the rapid changes of the twenty-first century.

In our struggle to remain significant we have gone from an age of church growth that aligned with the mantra "If you build it, they will come" to a new mantra of "If you have the right type of worship, they will come." When these strategies failed, we convinced ourselves that we needed to do church better: we needed to treat people like consumers and customers. Thus the church embraced business models like *Quest for Quality* and *Good To Great*.[1] Yet these business models were doomed

---

1. Collins, *Good to Great*.

to failure because they lacked religious and spiritual grounding. In other words, these business approaches failed because they were human programs lacking the *missio Dei.*

Today's Christian leaders need to believe that what we do is a God movement, not a human program. We are not leaders that are in place just to provide solutions and strategies with predefined ends, but rather, as the authors of *Missional Leader* observed, we are to be leaders who "cultivate the practice of indwelling Scripture and discovering places for experiment and risk as people discover that the Spirit of God's life-giving future in Jesus is among them."[2]

In our desperate attempt to remain relevant, pastors and denominational leaders have lost touch with that which makes us relevant, the Holy Spirit. We have lost the art of cultivating a Holy Spirit-rich environment. We have lost touch with what the Spirit of God is doing in our church, in our communities and in our world. We have lost touch with our Wesleyan roots and with our own *Book of Discipline*'s call to live with "active expectancy."[3]

To be cultivators of a Holy Spirit–rich environment, we first must teach our church members and congregations to live with "active expectancy." *The Book of Discipline* describes Servant Ministry and Servant leadership this way: "*Mission as Active Expectancy*—The ministry of all Christians consists of service for the mission of God in the world. The mission of God is best expressed in the prayer Jesus taught his first disciples: Thy kingdom come; thy will be done, on earth as it is in heaven. All Christians, therefore, are to live in active expectancy: faithful in service of God and their neighbor; faithful in waiting for the fulfillment of God's universal love, justice and peace on earth as in heaven."[4] Living a life of active expectancy is shaped by the teachings of Jesus Christ and active cooperation with the Holy Spirit.

Living with active expectancy is something I grew up with as an African American raised in an African American United Methodist Church. When we gathered for worship, we expected the Holy Spirit to show up. We expected the singing and the preaching to be Holy Spirit inspired. We expected our lives and our decisions to be Holy Spirit inspired.

2. Roxburgh and Romanuk, *The Missional Leader,* 27.

3. Alexander et al., *The Book of Discipline,* 91.

4. Ibid.

Unfortunately, as an African American district superintendent dealing with Anglo congregations, I have found that there is very little expectation that the Holy Spirit will be active in their worship or their decisions.

Many of these churches have lost touch with the *missio Dei,* the divine movement of God, and have become places of human programs designed to reflect spiritual and religious values—but in reality, they reflect a dying church out of touch with the life giving Spirit of God. In these churches, the Holy Spirit is a theological and intellectual construct, not a divine reality.

As Christian leaders in the Methodist and Wesleyan tradition we are called to be "head and heart" people. We are called to cultivate environments where thinking people can expect and experience the strange and wonderful "warming of the heart." Towards this end, Kelsey, in her paper, discusses two foundational practices for leadership within Christian communities of faith. She first asserts that leaders must practice daily prayer, which leads to the cultivation of careful listening to God's Holy Spirit. Her second assertion is that leaders who listen deeply to the Holy Spirit will be led to listen deeply to persons in their communities whose life experience is very different from their own. As Christian leaders listen to people in their communities, they will begin to see how the Spirit is at work in those communities and how they can lead Christian faith communities to participate in what the Holy Spirit is doing.

Kelsey's observations about the Holy Spirit and Christian leadership are in line with my individual and professional practices. As such, I want to briefly conclude with the foundational practices that make up my current ministry as a district superintendent.

One of the ways I pray and listen to the Holy Spirit is through the practice of *lectio divina. Lectio divina* literally means "divine reading." It is the practice of reading and praying the Scripture. In *lectio divina* you read a Scripture text from the Bible several times and listen with the ear of the heart to what God is saying to you in this moment of prayer. The movements of *lectio divina* are *lectio,* moments of reading the Scripture passage; *meditatio,* reflecting on the Scripture passage and listening for words or phrases that the Holy Spirit is directing you to pay attention to; *oratio,* responding to the Spirit's direction; and *contemplatio,* resting in the Word of God. The goal of *lectio divina* is to cultivate the practice of listening to the Holy Spirit with the aim of nourishing and deepening your relationship with God. *Lectio divina* takes you inward to listen to the

Holy Spirit and then it prepares you to participate in what God is doing in the world through the Holy Spirit.

When the bishop's cabinet (all the conference district superintendents) meets, we start our day with the group prayer practice of *lectio divina*. As a way of cultivating leaders who will cultivate a Spirit-rich environment, the Rocky Mountain Conference has contracted with Alan Roxburgh, author of *The Missional Leader*, to work with each district superintendent to create, train, and facilitate small groups of clergy leaders as Missional Leaders. *Lectio divina* using the Scripture of Luke 10:1–12 is a major part of this training.

As each leader progresses in the missional leader training, they will begin to cultivate an environment in their churches that leads to church members learning to listen and discern the movement of the Holy Spirit in their lives and in the community around them. The ultimate goal is twofold: first, to learn to live in "active expectancy" as we discern the movement of the Holy Spirit in our lives and in our communities, and second, to listen to the needs of people in our churches and in the communities around our churches so that we not only discern what the Holy Spirit is doing but that we actively participate with the Spirit, as a response to the needs of the people, and thus bring about the reality of God's Kingdom on earth. If the church can accomplish these two goals, she will reemerge from the crisis of creeping irrelevance and, once again, establish herself as a God movement and not a human program. When we claim with authenticity that we are a God movement, not a human program, and we demonstrate this by actively cooperating with what God is doing in the world through the Holy Spirit, we will squash the creeping specter of irrelevance because the church will be relevant to the people of the twenty-first century.

With this vision of a strong Spirit-filled church, I lift up this prayer, "Come Holy Spirit, Come and enliven your people and your church again!"

---

## BIBLIOGRAPHY

Alexander, Neil M. et al., editors. *The Book of Discipline of the United Methodist Church, 2008.* Nashville: The United Methodist Publishing House, 2008.

Collins, James. *Good to Great: Why Some Companies Make the Leap—and Others Don't.* New York: HarperBusiness, 2001.

Roxburgh, Alan J., and Fred Romanuk. *The Missional Leader: Equipping Your Church to Reach a Changing World.* San Francisco: Jossey-Bass, 2006.

# PART TWO

## Women and Ministry

# Chapter Four

## Preaching as an Art of Shared Leadership

### Eunjoo Mary Kim

A COUPLE YEARS AGO, I had an interesting conversation with a friend of mine who is a lay leader of her church. She expressed her disappointment with her new pastor's preaching. Her major complaint was that in his preaching, he treated his listeners like little children inferior to him in knowledge and experience and considered them the object rather than the subject of his ministry. However, she comforted herself by telling me that her church would be fine with that pastor as long as he could perform other leadership roles effectively, for preaching might be just one of the components of pastoral leadership. Recently, I met her again and learned that her church was in crisis because of the pastor's lack of leadership. That time, she firmly declared that "Preaching is not merely *a* component of pastoral leadership but is itself leadership!"

"Preaching is itself pastoral leadership!" This statement may sound exaggerated since the pastoral role is multifaceted. It makes sense, however, when we realize that preaching represents the particular style of a pastor's leadership and that preaching is the most important medium of communication between the pastor and the congregation. Through preaching, pastors regularly communicate spiritual and pastoral concerns in public and provide theological and practical directions for the journey of the community of faith on personal and communal levels. Upon realizing the inseparable relationship between preaching and church leadership, the preacher needs to ask such crucial questions as these: What does leadership mean for the church in our changing context for the ministry? What kind of paradigm shift is necessary for the ministry of preaching in order to participate in the renewed leadership of the church? How can the church practice theologically relevant and practically appropriate preaching?

This essay seeks to answer these questions by proposing a new paradigm of preaching based on a new leadership model. Concerning the search for a new leadership model, historian Jean Miller Schmidt reminds us of a lesson from church history, that the ministry of female preachers in early American Methodism thrived because of "the vital partnership in ministry between laity and clergy-lay preachers and class leaders providing pastoral leadership at the local level."[1] Further, she tells us that partnership between clergy and laity grounded in the "ultimate trust in the sufficiency of grace" of God was the foundation of church leadership in early American Methodism.[2]

These historical remarks of Schmidt's will be the starting point for developing a new paradigm of preaching in the following five sections of the essay. The first section will focus on understanding the context for preaching by analyzing internal and external conditions of the contemporary church. The second section will be a brief historical review of leadership in the church, paying special attention to the practice of the shared ministry. The third section will explore the theological meaning of leadership in light of shared ministry and will propose shared leadership as a new leadership model for the renewal of preaching. The fourth section will concentrate on the understanding of preaching as a practice of the shared ministry. The last section will focus on developing the practice of preaching as an art of shared leadership by suggesting a practical theological methodology.

1. Schmidt, *Grace Sufficient*, 151.
2. Ibid., 21.

## Preaching in Transition

The development of a new paradigm of preaching should begin with "exegeting" the congregation. As Leonora T. Tisdale urges in her book *Preaching as Local Theology and Folk Art*, preaching requires the preacher to exegete both the biblical text and the congregational culture.[3] However, the congregational culture is not merely formed by internal cultural components but is also exposed to the larger world to which the congregation belongs. Obviously, contemporary churches are facing complex internal and external conditions in many unpredicted ways. Just as our society is going through phenomenal spiritual, political, and sociocultural shifts, so are Christian churches. Such shifts can be explained in at least three ways.

First of all, one of the most challenging internal conditions of the church is the enhancement of egalitarianism in the leadership roles of the church. Since the middle of the twentieth century, mainstream churches in the United States have gradually begun to ordain women to the role of Minister of the Word and Sacrament and have allowed them to serve the church as lay leaders. Currently, about fifteen Protestant denominations allow women to be ordained pastors, and a growing number of female clergy serve local churches as Ministers of the Word and Sacrament. For example, 23 percent of United Methodist Church clergy are now female.[4] In the 2006 statistics of the Presbyterian Church (USA), women comprise approximately 30 percent of active (nonretired) clergy.[5] The Evangelical Lutheran Church in America reports that the percentage of its ordained clergywomen doubled from 1991 to 2003, to 16 percent.[6]

Many clergy in mainstream churches—both female and male—experience traditional patriarchal leadership as no longer effective in the contemporary context of the ministry. This kind of experience challenges church leaders to reconsider the concept of leadership and seek a more egalitarian and collaborative leadership model. If the leadership model

---

3. Tisdale, *Preaching as Local Theology and Folk Art*.

4. *General Commission on the Status and Role of Women*. Online: http://www.gcsrw.org/.

5. Presbyterian Church (USA), "News and Announcements" (2006). Online: http://www.pcusa.org/pcnews/2006/06538.htm/.

6. Evangelical Lutheran Church in America, "Welcome to the ELCA." Online: http://www.elca.org/Who-We-Are/Welcome-to-the-ELCA.aspx/.

changes in this way, the ministry of preaching also needs to change, since it is closely related to the practice of leadership in the church.

Another shift in the mainstream church that challenges the traditional model of church leadership is its membership decline.[7] The heyday of large memberships in mainstream churches has passed. Half a century ago, mainline denominations were bursting at the seams. They were so thriving that their church buildings were on every corner of the streets, and many of their churches were so affluent that they could offer a luxurious salary and benefit package to pastors. Nowadays, however, many churches struggle to pay ordained pastors even their minimum compensations required by their denominations. As a result, they cannot help but replace paid staff positions with lay volunteers and encourage lay people to participate in leadership roles which were once played by professionally trained pastoral leaders. The increasing demand on lay leadership challenges both clergy and laity to reconsider the identity and mission of the church and to ponder how to develop shared leadership between clergy and laity, not merely for their churches to survive but to thrive in the changing situation.

Shared leadership is also more demanding when we realize the shift of our world into an age of globalization. In our globalized world, human beings and other creatures are interconnected beyond geographical boundaries, more closely than ever before in human history. The global economy and the advancement of communication technology and transportation systems have contributed to changing our society into multicultural and multiracial environments. Moreover, the local is no longer isolated from the global. On a daily basis, people are experiencing social and ethical issues in their local contexts that emerge from the larger context of the globe.

In our increasingly multicultural society in North America, many churches realize that they can no longer remain homogenous in regards to race, ethnicity, language, and culture and therefore face practical issues such as whether they give up on their racial and cultural homogeneity

7. See Hout et al., "Demographics of Mainline Decline"; The Presbyterian Church (USA) lost 46,544 members (2 percent) in 2006 and 57, 572 members (2.5 percent) in 2007 (blog.gajunkie.com/ . . . /pcusa-membership-statistics-for-2007.aspx/, viewed on 08/12/2010); the United Methodist Church lost 1.01 percent of professing membership in 2008 (www.umc.org/site/apps/nlnet/content3.aspx?c...b=2789393/; viewed on 08/12/2010); the Episcopal Church membership has declined 7 percent and Sunday attendance by 11 percent over the past five years (geoconger.wordpress.com/ . . . /more-pressure-to-postpone-lambeth-conference-on-110907-p-6/; viewed on 08/12/2010).

and open to become an inclusive community or move to a less multiracial location to keep their traditionally homogeneous identity. It is unrealistic, however, to try to escape the changing reality entirely. The more we are aware of the web of interconnectedness we share with others, the more we understand that diversity is one of the crucial issues for the church to deal with. The issue of diversity challenges the leaders of the church to reconsider its identity and how to share leadership with others who are racially and culturally different from them.

In the changing context for preaching caused by such internal and external conditions as egalitarianism, membership change, and globalization, pastors are challenged to reconsider the concept of leadership and to reevaluate their ministry of preaching as a practice of their leadership. Leadership in the Christian community is inherently a matter of communication.[8] Through many different forms of communication, the vision and mission of the church are renewed, and the attitude and behavior of the members are transformed to live out the shared vision of their church. Therefore, the leadership of the church is broader than the official leaders of the church. It is a shared exercise of influence between the pastor and the congregation.

Keeping in mind this understanding of leadership, following is a brief review of the exercise of leadership in the church. Critical reflection on the history of church leadership will provide us with insights into developing a new leadership model which can bring a paradigm shift in preaching for our contemporary church.

## A Historical Review of Church Leadership[9]

The history of the primitive and early churches reminds us that the Christian church was first formed by means of the shared ministry. The Acts of the Apostles, Pauline letters, and Pastoral Epistles in the New Testament are evidence that the original model of the Christian ministry was a shared ministry between traveling apostles and local church leaders. In addition to the historical records, biblical references of such metaphors as the body whose parts have different functions for its organism

8. Osmer, *Practical Theology*, 26.

9. Some portion of this section is included in my essay, "Asian American Women and Renewal of Preaching," in which the initial idea of the paradigm of preaching as a shared ministry was explored.

(Rom 12:4ff; 1 Cor 12:12ff) and house utensils that are made for different purposes (2 Tim 2:20–22) show that primitive churches were encouraged to share ministry based on the gifts that members were granted by God. Early church history also reveals dynamic interaction among members of the church in a wide variety of leadership roles such as preachers, apostles, deacons, teachers, prophets, and priests, regardless of gender, race, and social status.[10]

Since the church was institutionalized under the Roman Empire, however, church leadership has belonged solely to clergy. Through the process of institutionalization, the church created hierarchical leadership positions and limited them to educated male clergy. The shift of church leadership from shared to clergy-centered ministry has changed the concept of the ministry in terms of clericalism and degraded the role of the laity into passive recipients of the ministry. Yet, the clergy-centered patriarchal orders of church ministry were protested by numerous ecclesial movements during the medieval era. Many female leaders and laymen resisted the hierarchical system of the church and struggled against it to regain equal opportunities to participate in church leadership beyond the boundaries of gender, race, education, and class. For example, from the end of the twelfth century to the early thirteenth century, the Carthars and Waldensians in the south of France, in Italy, in Flanders, and in certain areas of the Rhine Valley revolted against the established orders of the church and claimed that church leadership, especially the right to preach, should be open to the laity.[11]

Martin Luther, John Calvin, and other sixteenth-century reformers also denied the ecclesial orders and reclaimed the authority and right of the laity to participate in church leadership. They proposed the shared leadership of the primitive church in the New Testament as the ideal for the Reformed church. It is noteworthy that among the reformers, Calvin was not an ordained minister but still played a dominant role in the leadership of the Reformed church. He served the church by preaching, teaching, and administering sacraments, never wanting to be an ordained pastor, for he firmly believed that ordination "was not an indispensable requirement for serving God's Word and leading the community" and that the pastoral office should be functional "under the working of God's

10. Kim, *Women Preaching*, 34–35.

11. Ibid., 53.

Spirit."[12] Yet, Calvin and other reformers restricted their understanding and practice of the shared ministry to men. A number of Pietist groups, however, such as Mennonites, Quakers, and Baptists, emerging later outside the mainstream of the Reformed Church, extended the reformers' doctrines of Christian freedom and the priesthood of all believers to women and included them in their shared leadership.[13]

Shared ministry was also revived in the early Methodist movement in the eighteenth century. Wesleyan theology emphasizing the freedom of the Holy Spirit and its personal experience as the source of individual and communal transformation became the theological foundation for the movement to view the church as functional and charismatic rather than institutional and authoritarian. Such theological understandings of the church diluted the boundary line between women and men as well as that between clergy and laity in leadership roles. Most of all, due to the undersupply of ordained clergy to the expansion of the movement, the leaders of the movement could not help but share their leadership roles with the laity and even with women. During Wesley's late days, women were granted the right to preach and, as a result, many Methodist women participated in preaching as well as leading class meetings and love feasts. The vital partnership in ministry between clergy and laity made it possible for the Methodist movement to grow to become an independent denomination of the Christian church.[14]

In nineteenth-century America, however, the Methodist church was institutionalized by male leaders and failed to embrace women and racially marginalized people in the leadership of the church. More precisely, just twelve years after Wesley's death in 1791, the majority of conservative male leaders resolved to rule women's preaching unnecessary and, consequently, few Methodist women could share the pulpit with male preachers from that point in time until the middle of the twentieth century.[15] Furthermore, African American converts who were former slaves were excluded from the leadership roles of the church and eventually separated

---

12. McKim, *Cambridge Companion to John Calvin*, 10.

13. Kim, *Women Preaching*, 80, 84–85.

14. Kim, *Women Preaching*, 151.

15. Ibid., 88.

themselves to establish an independent Christian church, the African Methodist Episcopal Church, in 1815.[16]

Shared ministry is biblical and powerful. But most churches have ignored its theological and practical significance, keeping the status quo of the traditional model of clergy-centered patriarchal leadership as the standard of church leadership. Against this situation, the movement of feminist theology since the middle of the twentieth century has raised a prophetic voice. In her book *Church in the Round: Feminist Interpretation of the Church*, Letty Russell regrets clerical privilege in the leadership of the church[17] and urges leaders of the church to revive the "partnership paradigm" of church leadership. As a way to share ministry with the laity, Russell proposes "round table leadership."[18] According to Russell, round table leadership is centered in "Spirit-filled communities" rather than privileged individuals and shares "the gifts of the Spirit among all those who share new life in Christ."[19] In round table leadership, power and authority are "something to be multiplied and shared rather than accumulated at the top."[20] Therefore, "there are never too many leaders, for power is not understood as a zero sum game that requires competition and hoarding in order to 'win.' Rather, power and leadership gifts multiply as they are shared and more and more persons become partners in communities of faith and struggle."[21]

Today, this feminist understanding of church leadership cannot be taken as a marginalized voice in theological education. Rather, it is essential to revitalize contemporary churches. Many theologians and church leaders who take seriously the changing context for the ministry agree that traditional clergy-centered patriarchal leadership is no longer a relevant leadership model for the church and that the partnership model, which has already been proposed by feminist theologians and church leaders, should be the paradigm of a new leadership model of the church.

For example, in his book *As One with Authority: Reflective Leadership in Ministry*, Jackson W. Carroll proposes "reflective leadership" as a new

16. African Methodist Episcopal Church, "About Us." Online: http://www.ame-church.com/about-us/history.php/.

17. Russell, *Church in the Round*, 54.

18. Ibid., 63.

19. Ibid., 64.

20. Ibid., 57.

21. Ibid., 56.

leadership model. In reflective leadership, explains Carroll, leaders function not in "a top-down, asymmetrical fashion"[22] but invite their congregants to be their ministry partners in the process of "reflection-in-action."[23] As another example, Norma Cook Everist and Craig L. Nessan propose the "relational leadership" model. In their book *Transforming Leadership: New Vision for a Church in Mission*, they emphasize the significance of a "genuine partnership between the called leader and all of the people" and suggest that church leadership should be relational between pastoral leaders and their congregants in order to bring forth a mutual transformation between them, thus participating in God's mission of justice and peace.[24]

In addition, Richard L. Hamm develops the concept of shared leadership into the practice of team ministry. In his book *Recreating the Church: Leadership for the Postmodern Age*, Hamm analyzes complex problems associated with leadership in the contemporary church and proposes that team ministry based on relationship and trust between the clergy and laity should be a way to recreate the church. For Hamm, ministry with a team of people who have complementary leadership styles makes it possible to bring changes into the church, since the team can explore what changes are necessary and how it can seek these changes in an approach relevant to the internal and external situation of their church.[25]

## Preaching and the Theology of Shared Leadership

The phenomenological analysis of our context for preaching and the critical review of church leadership throughout its history convince us that the leadership model for our contemporary church should be shifted from the traditional patriarchal leadership model to the shared leadership model. However, shared leadership seems unrealistic when it relates to the ministry of preaching. On the one hand, most mainstream Christian churches firmly believe that only professionally educated clergy can preach. On the other hand, preaching has been understood as one of the most power-related ministries. Many pastors who were raised in the environment of clerical elitism tend to regard preaching as their distinctive privilege and right that they should not give up. In addition, they are

22. Carroll, *One with Authority*, first ed., 123.
23. Ibid., 177.
24. Everist and Nessan, *Transforming Leadership*, viii–ix.
25. Hamm, *Recreating the Church*, 91–94.

afraid that their congregations may judge them impotent if they share their preaching ministry with others. Consequently, the pulpit has been the most exclusive place, in which serious leadership issues are tangled. In an actual ministerial context, for example, how the pulpit can be shared between the senior pastor, who is usually male, and the associate pastor, who is usually female, is one of the tricky issues, let alone how to share the pulpit with the laity.

Nonetheless, it is crucial to reconsider the practice of preaching in relation to shared leadership, for it is theological rather than simply pragmatic. The concept of shared leadership is grounded in "the intercommunion of our Triune God," who is "by nature relational."[26] The relational life of God revealed in the Trinity should be the source and the goal of church leadership. The relationality of God in the Trinitarian structure means that the nature of God is not a single being manifesting oneself in various forms but that which pervades and reaches beyond a single entity to include others in its oneness, which is "the communal principle."[27] In the Divine communality, the three Persons are ontologically equal, and there are no hierarchical degrees among them. Each Person of the Trinity is seen as God who shares in the fullness of the substance and has difference in its function. But different functions of the three Persons do not make them superior or inferior to others but make God's nature interdependent among the three Persons. Thus, the unity of the Trinity is defined in terms of the community which the members of the Trinity share. That is, the fundamental unity of God is "a unity-in-difference."[28]

In the divine community, power is the one thing shared among the members, for it is not the possession of a singular Person but belongs to the essential nature or substance of what it means to be Divine. In other words, God shares power with the three Persons on the ontological level and makes it a force for the Divine, who is in essence a fundamentally active principle in or a force to the universe.[29] God's nature endlessly shares God's providential power among the three Persons through the way that is faithful to God's essence, love, and character, the *kenosis*, revealed in Jesus Christ (Philippians 2:11). Since God is love, God restricts God's own

---

26. Everist and Nessan, *Transforming Leadership*, 4.

27. Ogbonnaya, *Communitarian Divinity*, 77.

28. Jansen, *Relationality*, 110.

29. Ibid., 82.

power and presence to allow creation to exist and shares power among creatures to whom God relates through the *kenosis*, self-emptying. God, who interacts with God's creation not by subordination and servitude but by mutuality and love, necessarily requires the freedom of human beings to respond to this love.[30]

If God's nature is understood as relational and communal, the relationship between God and God's creatures is to be reciprocal and mutual. Moreover, relationships among God's creatures should be based on reciprocity and mutuality. Just as the nature and power of God is correlative with the three Persons in the Trinity, so we humans are created to live out the image of the relational God through sharing our gifts and power granted by God. When those gifts and power are shared among the members of the church in trust of the guidance of the Holy Spirit, the church flourishes best toward mutual transformation among its members.

The theological ground of shared leadership in the Trinitarian structure of God challenges us to rethink the nature and practice of preaching. Throughout church history, the pulpit has been the place of demonstrating God's power, and many Christians have imagined who God is based on the preacher's exercise of power behind the pulpit. If God's nature is relational by sharing the divine power among the three Persons and among the creatures, our preaching should also be relational in order to appropriately represent the nature and power of God. That is, the pulpit should no longer be the place of a monopoly on power, but must be a place representing God's relational nature and shared power to the world.

The exercise of power behind the pulpit can be transformed into this Trinitarian way when the traditional patriarchal paradigm of preaching is shifted to the paradigm of preaching as a shared ministry beyond clericalism. Preaching as a shared ministry is a practice of shared leadership based on open, inclusive, and communal relationships with others. Such preaching shares the authority and power with others, not only collegial people but also traditionally underrepresented groups in the church based on gender, sexuality, social and economic status, race and ethnicity. The new paradigm of preaching as a shared ministry will freely invite those who are willing to witness to God's redemptive power in their lives and creatively work in collaboration to transform the church and the larger world into a place where people can foretaste God's reign.

30. Ibid., 127.

## Preaching as a Shared Ministry

Preaching as a practice of shared leadership is a communal effort between the pastor and the congregation to discern God's grace in their lives together and bring it into a shared experience. As Schmidt reminds us, "there is grace sufficient even for our day,"[31] and the more the pulpit is open, inclusive, and communal, the more can God's grace be discerned and shared with others.

In order to practice preaching as a shared ministry, at least four prerequisites are necessary. The first is that the pastor and the congregation should reconstruct their understanding of authority. Traditionally, authority has been perceived as the power of control possessed by the person who stands on top of a hierarchical system. Such an understanding, however, is not the authentic meaning of authority, because authority is in essence relational, rather than hierarchical, rooted in God, who is its ultimate source. More precisely, God has granted authority to people in manifold ways "as abundant commodity"[32] or gifts to share with others. Authority in the church, therefore, is not a possession that the leader should make every effort not to lose in competition with others but God's gift that is supposed to be shared with others as a means of building up the community of faith (cf. Eph 4:7–12).

In her book *Growing in Authority: Relinquishing Control*, Celia Allison Hahn explores the multiplicity of exercising authority and categorizes it into four different modes: received authority (shaped in roles they receive), autonomous authority (shaped by professional knowledge and experience), assertive authority (shaped by relationship with other), and integrated authority (shaped by using the above three modes of authority contextually and eclectically). Among Hahn's description of the four modes of authority, integrated authority provides insight into understanding authority in relation to the practice of preaching as a shared ministry. According to Hahn, integrated authority emerges in paradox between the authority coming from within the self of the leader and the willingness to share her authority with others and arrives at "a paradoxical and gratifying resolution of the self-other contradictions"[33] by setting aside for a time her received authority and giving up some of her autonomy and assertiveness

31. Schmidt, *Grace Sufficient*, 295.

32. Hahn, *Growing in Authority*, 27.

33. Ibid., 90.

for the sake of the people she is called to serve.[34] If pastors understand their authority as integrated authority, they will not consider their preaching as a win-lose game, competing with others, but a shared ministry with others for mutual growth. By sharing preaching, pastors can provide hospitable space in which others can participate in discerning the grace of God and empower one another to blossom God's abundant authority among them.

The second prerequisite for the practice of preaching as a shared ministry is that both the pastor and lay leaders should have a humble mind or humility. N. Graham Standish may be right when he regrets that "too many churches have pastoral and lay leaders who are somewhat arrogant, assuming they always know what is best and that the members are spiritual infants who are ignorant of God's desires."[35] How, then, can such church leaders open themselves to God and others and submit themselves to their wisdom? Only genuine humility makes it possible. Genuine humility means neither condescendence nor impotence but honest openness to God and others with respect to diversity. Respect is a "willingness to show consideration or appreciation for someone"[36] who has a different value-orientation and life-experience. By respecting difference, pastors and lay leaders can place their egos at the service of others.

Genuine humility leads pastors to realize that preaching is a communal calling, a calling to an interdependent and collaborative partnership with others. By humbly praying and studying together with others—especially the marginalized, oppressed, and exploited–to discern God's mysterious presence and power in our mundane lives and by sharing them with others through preaching, the pastor can help the congregation freely witness to God's grace to the world. Consequently, preaching as a collaborative ministry contributes to transforming the church, whose "'product' is transformed people."[37]

The third prerequisite for the practice of preaching as a shared ministry is that the pastor should have a teachable spirit and pedagogical skills to train and work with her preaching partners. Some may think that shared preaching will result in a negligence of the pastor's responsibility as a preacher and an exploitation of the labor of lay people or other staff

34. Ibid., 24.

35. Standish, *Humble Leadership*, 17.

36. Everist and Nessan, *Transforming Leadership*, 123.

37. Hahn, *Growing in Authority*, 116.

members to lighten the burden of the pastor's duty of preaching. Or, the practice of preaching as a shared ministry may lead to a misconception that it does not take seriously preachers' education or training because shared preaching invites every believer to participate in preaching regardless of one's qualifications.

However, these are not true. Shared preaching demands of the pastor not only her sufficient knowledge and experience of preaching but also her passion and diligent efforts to sustain the pulpit to be the place where God's truthful message is communicated in quality. This is not possible without the pastor's willingness and ability to educate her preaching partners to be faithful witnesses to the Word. From the selection of a preaching partner(s) through the process of sermon preparation and to the performance of preaching, the pastor should be the leader of the shared ministry of preaching by teaching, facilitating, directing, and encouraging her preaching partners. Thus, the image of the pastor for the practice of preaching as a shared ministry is multiple, including the images of a teacher, a facilitator, a colleague, a coach, a project coordinator, and, most of all, the leader of the congregation. Through these leadership roles, the pastor is called for "the equipping of the saints for the work of ministry" (Eph 4:12). The pastor serves those whom she is called to lead by helping them participate in witnessing to the grace of God to and beyond the church.

The last prerequisite for the practice of preaching as a shared ministry is that the pastor should have skills for building up relationships with others. The church is a covenantal community, formed based on relationships with God and with people and continuously renews its identity, vision, and mission through preaching and other ministries. While contractual relationships are concerned with job descriptions, compensation, working conditions, and such like, covenantal relationships are concerned with the right of the members to be involved in both the ownership of problems and responsibility for the community, i.e., the right to make a commitment to the community. In order for people to feel a sense of belonging in the covenantal community, a great deal of trust among the members of the community and a clear sense of interdependence between the leader and the members are eminently necessary.[38]

---

38. De Pree, *Leadership Is an Art*, 36–43.

The church, like other covenantal communities, is based on the commitment of the members, and they assume a genuine opening of the community to their influence by letting them use their gifts in decision making, implementation, and evaluation of community events. Thus, leadership for the church does not depend on the pastor's tactics or strategies but artful skills of relationships, including creativity in attentiveness to the divine action already present in individual and communal lives and pastoral skills in listening to people and polishing, liberating, and enabling the gifts that they bring to the church. Preaching can be practiced as a shared ministry when the pastor has an ability to perform this kind of art; the pastor who is willing to practice preaching as a shared ministry is called to be an artist who builds relationships with God and the people.

## Preaching and Practical Theology

*Shared ministry* is a comprehensive term that means a collaborative ministry between leaders of the church and its members. If we consider preaching a shared ministry, how can preaching be practiced in an actual ministerial setting? While a wide range of practices can be experimented with in creative ways, it is important to remember that the practice of preaching as a shared ministry is a practical theological discipline. Just as preaching is a subdiscipline of practical theology, so is preaching as a shared ministry.

In the contemporary theological education system designed on the basis of the clear-cut dichotomy between theory and practice, the term practical theology tends to be regarded as an "applied theology," whose aim is to teach students techniques and skills of application of the substance that were gained in other fields such as biblical, historical, and systematic theologies. Practical theology, however, is more than "a handmaid of other theologies," for it means a dynamic theological reflection that guides the church to the life of faith. It includes all doctrinal and biblical teachings and metaphysical reflections about God related directly to the life of faith and offers pastoral and soteriological implications for the daily lives of believers. In fact, Christian theology is, in its origin, not abstract or speculative but a "practical discipline" that concerns a vital relationship between theological reflection and the practice of a Christian life in the world. In other words, all Christian theology is, in essence, practical theology, for, as H. Richard Niebuhr insists, all theological reflection is inherently practical and, in this sense, all theology is practical.[39]

The subject of practical theology is not restricted to ordained ministers but includes all believers—both clergy and laity. As a community, the entire congregation is responsible for theological reflection on their practice. Here, the term practice does not mean a simple application of theory but "practical wisdom" or "*phronesis*" in Aristotle's term. Its definition is a "prudent understanding of variable situations with a view as to what is to be done."[40] Moreover, practice is not an activity of a single person, but a communal activity which creates a new way of life in the context of a community.

The holistic and communal aspect of practical theology can be described no better than in the way Friedrich Schleiermacher does. Although Schleiermacher divides areas of studying Christian theology into three— philosophical, historical, and practical—he stresses practical theology as "the crown of theological study." For him, "leadership in the church is the final purpose of theology," and the area of practical theology is "the final part of the study because it prepares for direct action."[41] Therefore, all theological knowledge taught in the areas of philosophical, biblical, and historical theologies must be reflected in relation to our personal and communal lives to give meaning and direction to the present and future lives of humanity.

Schleiermacher further suggests that the method of practical theology should be a "probing, rigorous, critical, and constructive" theological reflection, stepping back to think about the meaning of faith, church, and life, with some critical distance before again jumping into action.[42] This reflective method has been advanced by contemporary practical theologians such as Richard R. Osmer. In his book *Practical Theology: An Introduction,* Osmer develops the method of practical theological reflection into four interpretive tasks, based on the reciprocal relationship between theory and practice: 1) the descriptive-empirical task, 2) the interpretive task, 3) the normative task, and 4) the pragmatic task. In the stage of the descriptive-empirical task, the pastor gathers information

39. Niebuhr, *Radical Monotheism*, 115–16.

40. Tracy, "Foundations of Practical Theology," 73.

41. Schleiermacher, *Christian Caring*, 99.

42. Ibid., 17.

about the context for the ministry "through informal information gathering, careful listening and looking more closely at patterns and relationships that are taken for granted," by asking, "What is going on?" In the stage of the interpretive task, the pastor goes deeper to better understand patterns and dynamics occurring in the particular situation by analyzing them through theories of the arts and sciences, by asking, "Why is this going on?" In the stage of the normative task, the pastor uses theological concepts to interpret particular episodes, situations, or contexts, constructing ethical norms to guide our responses and learning from "good practice," by asking, "What ought to be going on?" In the last stage of the pragmatic task, the pastor determines strategies of action that will influence situations in ways that are desirable and enter into a reflective conversation with the "talk back" emerging when they are enacted, by asking, "How might we respond?"[43] For Osmer, this interpretive process is more like a "spiral" than a circle, since it constantly circles back to tasks that have already been explored.[44]

Preaching as a shared ministry should be practiced not as a random or arbitrary case study but as a consistent practical theological act followed by critical reflection. Osmer's four core tasks of interpretation for practical theological reflection can be used as guidelines for the practice of preaching as a shared ministry. For example, the history and current situation of the preaching ministry in a particular church can be analyzed through the descriptive-empirical and the interpretive tasks. The normative task will help the pastor theologically reflect on the current practice of preaching in her church and provide theological guidance for the practice of preaching as a shared ministry. And the pragmatic task will help the pastor discern her role as the leader of the shared ministry and increase her pastoral sensibility.

Through the process of practical theological reflection, the pastor can practice preaching as a shared ministry in a variety of ways. For some churches that understand preaching as the pastor's own business, a low-key introduction to shared preaching may be effective. Such churches may begin by inviting some lay leaders or staff members to preach a children's sermon in Sunday worship. Churches that have a Bible study program may develop it into a lectionary reading group or a theological book club,

43. Osmer, *Practical Theology*, 4–10.
44. Ibid,, 11.

in which the pastor can study with the members, focusing on some theological theme or preaching texts, and then reflect on the discussion later when she prepares a sermon.

In churches that are open to new things in relation to the ministry of preaching and had talented members in storytelling, music, dance, audiovisual technology, and so forth, the pastor can be creative in preparing preaching by inviting them to participate in the preaching event based on their talents. Preaching a dramatized sermon, a dialogue sermon, a theatrical sermon combined with music and dance, etc., can be rehearsed with a team in a given time and situation. Designing a sermon as a dialogue with preaching partner(s), rather than as a monologue by the pastor, or as an embodied performance including singing, drama, dancing, and other artistic elements by inviting those who have such talents among the congregation will help the congregation understand preaching as a shared ministry. For the effective practice of preaching as a shared ministry, it would be useful to organize a preaching committee, whose role is to participate not only in preparing, performing, and evaluating preaching but also in recruiting participants who are interested in sharing their experiences of God's grace with others through preaching.

The practice of preaching as a shared ministry is not limited to the preparation process and actual performance. It can be extended to post-preaching events such as a sermon feedback time after the service. Or, if a congregation is open and flexible to changes in the order of the worship service and is interested in sharing their reflections on the sermon during the service, the pastor can design the order of the service including a moment of reflection after the sermon as a response to the Word. This practice should be preceded by the pastor's instructions on how to share their responses to the sermon in constructive ways.

The ideas suggested above are just a few. The practice of preaching as a shared ministry requires of the preacher ongoing efforts to innovate and practice new ideas for shared preaching. A variety of creative approaches to preaching as a shared ministry will challenge the church to rethink its identity and mission and contribute to revitalizing the church with fresh insights and passion for communal and collaborative ministry. The practice of preaching as an art of shared leadership will eventually bring forth a new chapter of Christian ministry as an art through which the congregation can appreciate the beauty of leadership.

# BIBLIOGRAPHY

African Methodist Episcopal Church. "About Us—Our History." Online: http://www.ame-church.com/about-us/history.php/.

Carroll, Jackson W. *As One with Authority: Reflective Leadership in Ministry*. Louisville: Westminster John Knox, 1991.

———. *As One with Authority: Reflective Leadership in Ministry*. 2nd ed. Eugene, OR: Cascade Books, 2011.

Conger, George. "More Pressure to Postpone Lambeth Conference." Post on Conger (blog). November 11, 2007. Online: http://geoconger.wordpress.com/2007/11/11/more-pressure-to-postpone-lambeth-conference-cen-110907-p-7/

De Pree, Max. *Leadership Is an Art*. New York: Currency/Doubleday, 2004.

Evangelical Lutheran Church in America. "Welcome to the ELCA." Online: http://www.elca.org/Who-We-Are/Welcome-to-the-ELCA.aspx/.

Everist, Norma Cook, and Craig L. Nessan. *Transforming Leadership: New Vision for a Church in Mission*. Minneapolis: Fortress, 2008.

*General Commission on the Status and Role of Women*. Website. Online: http://www.gcsrw.org/.

Hahn, Celia Allison. *Growing in Authority, Relinquishing Control: A New Approach to Faithful Leadership*. Bethesda, MD: Alban Institute, 1994.

Hamm, Richard L. *Recreating the Church: Leadership for the Postmodern Age*. St. Louis: Chalice, 2007.

Hout, Michael, et al., "Demographics of Mainline Decline: Birth Dearth." *Christian Century*, October 4, 2005, 24–27.

Jansen, Henry. *Relationality and the Concept of God*. Currents of Encounter 10. Amsterdam: Rodopi, 1995.

Kim, Eunjoo Mary. "Asian American Women and Renewal of Preaching." In *New Feminist Christianity: Many Voices, Many Views*, edited by Mary E. Hunter and Diann L. Neu, 245–53. Woodstock, VT: Skylight Paths, 2010.

———. *Women Preaching: Theology and Practice through the Ages*. Cleveland: Pilgrim, 2004.

McKim, Donald K., editor. *The Cambridge Companion to John Calvin*. Cambridge Companions to Religion. Cambridge: Cambridge University Press, 2004.

Niebuhr, H. Richard. *Radical Monotheism and Western Culture*. New York: Harper & Row, 1960.

Ogbonnaya, A. Okechukwu. *On Communitarian Divinity: An African Interpretation of the Trinity*. New York: Paragon House, 1994.

Osmer, Richard R. *Practical Theology: An Introduction*. Grand Rapids: Eerdmans, 2008.

Presbyterian Church (USA). "News and Announcements." Online: http://www.pcusa.org/pcnews/2006/06538.htm/.

Russell, Letty. *Church in the Round: Feminist Interpretation of the Church*. Louisville: Westminster John Knox, 1993.

Schleiermacher, Friedrich. *Christian Caring: Selections from Practical Theology*. Edited with an introduction by James O. Duke and Howard Stone. Translated by James O. Duke. Fortress Texts in Modern Theology. Philadelphia: Fortress, 1988.

Schmidt, Jean Miller. *Grace Sufficient: A History of Women in American Methodism, 1760–1939*. Nashville: Abingdon, 1999.

Standish, N. Graham. *Humble Leadership: Being Radically Open to God's Guidance and Grace*. Herndon, VA: Alban Institute, 2007.

Tisdale, Leonora Tubbs. *Preaching as Local Theology and Folk Art*. Fortress Resources for Preaching. Minneapolis: Fortress, 1997.

Tracy, David. "The Foundations of Practical Theology." In *Practical Theology*, edited by Don Browning, 61–82. San Francisco: Harper & Row, 1983.

United Methodist Church. "Our Church." Online: http://www.umc.org/site/c. lwL4KnN1LtH/b.1355347/k.2F4F/Our_Church.htm/.

# Pastoral Response

## Holly Heuer

D R. KIM'S VISION OF shared preaching as a natural and theologically sound development of shared ministry is both provocative and in-spirational. Preaching has, indeed, been the last bastion of clergy pre-eminence. Church members seem to cherish the hierarchy of the pulpit, even in cases where they practice shared leadership in every other form. Without belaboring the causes or results of an exclusive claim that clergy have held on the pulpit, Dr. Kim invites a reconsideration of that assump-tion. She begins with the practical necessity for sharing preaching, but ultimately grounds her argument in the doctrine of the Trinity, where shared power clearly originates. Her suggestions for implementation of this vision—while challenging—are consistent with the high calling and art of the preaching enterprise.

We have engaged in some of the practices that Dr. Kim suggests in her section on practical theology. In our context at Calvary Presbyterian Church in Denver, Colorado, shared preaching has indeed grown out of years of shared ministry. Since Presbyterian polity requires shared leader-ship at all levels of the church's life, we are shaped by the required parity between elders and ministers. That being said, our *Book of Order* presumes an exclusive claim of clergy on the preaching event itself: "For reasons of order the preaching of the Word shall ordinarily be done by a minister of the Word and Sacrament" (W-2.2008). Presbyterian understanding of shared ministry means that we have separate roles: elders govern the church while pastors teach, administer sacraments, pray for the people, and preach. It has taken years of ministry together at Calvary for mutual trust to grow into real parity at all levels of ministry. Shared preaching has been a very gradual development. Liturgists have steadily expanded their skills and scope of worship leadership. Congregants have become more and more comfortable participating in dramatic readings of the text and even wearing costumes for seasonal dramas. Lay people have increasingly assumed significant responsibility for worship design. All of these were necessary steps in preparation for shared preaching.

Dr. Kim rightly assesses the necessary conditions for parity in the pulpit. Clergy must possess humility and a teachable spirit, and be willing to share authority. Those qualities may exist in one's early years of ministry, but in my experience, it takes time for such qualities to develop. In my early years of ministry, for example, I felt that I needed to prove myself, particularly in the area of preaching. It is not an easy art. I believe that before clergy can teach and encourage lay preaching, they need to have mastered those skills themselves. Thus, Dr. Kim's challenge is best heard by those who have both confidence and maturity in preaching.

As women move into places of leadership within the church, they bring a natural desire to relate as equals to their parishioners—opening up new possibilities for mutuality in the church. This shift is well documented by feminist theologians who have been on the frontier of shared partnership in ministry. Dr. Kim quotes Letty Russell in urging a return to the "partnership paradigm" that was established in the early years of the church's life. Russell calls for the church to return to its authentic roots, before its form was co-opted by the culture into a hierarchical monolithic institution. That call has been heard and heeded in some quarters of the church. But I believe that culture is a more powerful force in changing the customs of the church. As our wider society has been influenced by women's leadership, it has become more comfortable with an egalitarian model of leadership. The church is gradually following society's lead.

Like Dr. Kim, I find the doctrine of the Trinity to embody the clearest picture of mutuality, serving as both foundation and encouragement for a new paradigm for church leadership, and thus, preaching. In describing the Trinity, the Cappadocian fathers did not focus on the three discrete persons so much as on the relationship among them. In fact, as Cynthia Bourgeault writes, "The Cappadocians were interested in how this movement, or change of state, takes place. They saw it as an outpouring of love: from Father to Son, from Son to Spirit, from Spirit back to Father. And the word used to describe these mutual outpourings is . . . *kenosis*." She goes on to write, "The Trinity, understood in a wisdom sense, is really an icon of self-emptying love. The three persons go round and round like buckets on a watermill, constantly overspilling into one another. And as they do so, the mill turns and the energy of love becomes manifest and accessible."[1] This image of outpouring love, of shared partnership in the Godhead, is a profound model for the church's growing sense of itself. Shared ministry in all of its forms promises more than just a correction to the "proper" order of things. It promises a growth of love.

Calvary has experimented with a variety of ways of sharing preaching. I will describe a few of those forms, with my reflections on our experience. We have served as a teaching congregation for three intern pastors from the Iliff School of Theology. One of their privileges and responsibilities was preaching monthly. In each case, I worked with these students as they prepared their sermons—giving them feedback during a "practice" sermon and reflections following the worship service. Their lay committees also provided useful responses to their preaching. This investment in the students' growth developed a strong sense of mutuality, which deepened into bonds of love. The whole congregation was mobilized around the preaching event; it became the locus of a powerful outpouring of encouragement.

Members of the congregation have preached while I have been away and while I have been present. Occasionally I have preached a dialogue sermon with a lay person. On a couple of occasions we preached (as a congregation) a joint sermon. I provided the text and reflection questions several weeks ahead of time, adding ideas each week until the preaching day. Then, on the Sunday that the congregation preached, I provided a simple introduction to the text, and as people raised their hands, a microphone was brought to them and they spoke the gospel as they heard it. It was sometimes a bit messy, other times quite stimulating, and at still other times quite touching. But it deepened the awareness of the congregation of one another—their uniqueness and their value to the community of faith. And yes, love flowed. These occasions have generated a sense of appreciation for the "resident" wisdom of our congregation—developing a confidence in the accessibility of the gospel to lay people.

Another practice which has increased the "flow of love" is my weekly Bible study. Each Tuesday morning we study the text(s) that I will be

---

1. Bourgeault, *The Wisdom Jesus,* 71–72.

preaching on the following Sunday. Often I use quotes from the students in my sermon, so that their voice is included in the proclamation. On occasion I have invited them to weigh in: "So, what would you preach?" Every Bible student has found the sermon more meaningful, since they have tilled the soil of their own souls.

But the occasions of greatest excitement have been the many times that lay people have "witnessed" to the congregation. In our order of worship it is called "words of witness." It is not spontaneous, but a prepared message. We spend time with these lay people, helping them to hone their message, so that it is clear, authentic and relevant. These words have made a powerful mark on our community as people cherish these stories—and imagine their own.

It is easy when there is only one voice from the pulpit to assume that we are homogeneous and one-dimensional. Or even that the gospel is remote and inaccessible. Hearing many voices, we at Calvary have come to appreciate the gospel as an ongoing dialogue, a conversation within a congregation. And as we participate in that conversation, we receive and we pour ourselves out—in mutual encouragement and love.

---

# BIBLIOGRAPHY

Bourgeault, Cynthia. *The Wisdom Jesus: Transforming Heart and Mind—A New Perspective on Christ and His Message*. Boston: Shambhala, 2008.

Presbyterian Church (USA). *The Book of Order*, 2009–2011. Louisville: Office of the General Assembly, Presbyterian Church (U.S.A.), 2009.

# Chapter Five

## Drag and Other Practices of Unauthorized Leadership
### GLBT Persons Working for Social Change in the Church

### Katherine Turpin

O̲N̲ ̲T̲H̲E̲ ̲F̲I̲R̲S̲T̲ ̲S̲U̲N̲D̲A̲Y̲ morning in May, a local United Methodist congregation gathers for its regular weekly worship service. This service marks the congregation's third anniversary of becoming a member of the "Reconciling Ministries Network" within the United Methodist Church by making a public declaration of the congregation's full welcome to all persons of faith, including gay, lesbian, bisexual, and transgendered (GLBT) persons who are excluded by many Christian communities of faith. The occasion includes testimonies of faith from several of the congregation's members, the reaffirmation of the congregation's reconciling statement, the presence of rainbow colors throughout the sanctuary, and liturgies and prayers to re-affirm this element of the congregation's mission and identity.

Just prior to the celebration of communion, the pastor speaks briefly of her experiences at the United Methodist General Conference in the weeks prior to this service. As an alternate delegate, she has participated in many events and discussions at the conference dealing with the denomination's struggle regarding the full inclusion of GLBT persons as clergy persons. She tears up at various points in her description of the powerful events of the conference, including a ritual witness and protest on the floor of the fully assembled body in which she had taken part. As most of the congregation already knows, the denominational body has reaffirmed its exclusionary policies regarding the ordination of GLBT persons and refused to remove the language in *The Book of Discipline* that declares homosexuality "incompatible with Christian teaching." So, in this ritual moment, the congregation stands between its own celebration and witness to a commitment made and its grief and lament at belonging to a denomination that is not yet willing to witness to the wide circle of God's love in the same way.

This scene of celebration and lament would be poignant on its own for the congregation given its self-understanding and its sense of mission to witness to God's reconciling love. The depth of pain and contradiction embodied in this particular moment becomes even more evident if one realizes that the pastor, the very one about to break the bread and share the cup of Christ in this community, is a person involved in a committed same-sex relationship. By denominational standards, she is an impossibility, the very kind of person whose life the law of the church has declared incompatible with Christian teaching. Although she is careful to avoid publically declaring herself a "self-avowed, practicing homosexual" in order to prevent removal from her position and her long-term practice of ministry in the United Methodist Church, many of the members of the congregation know her partner and are aware of the personal pain caused by the decisions of the prior weeks. And yet, here she stands, leading the congregation in the sacramental practice, pastor and celebrant, despite the institutional structures and policies that would deny her service in this capacity.

## Closet or Drag? The Politics of Change from Within

I am a United Methodist layperson who teaches practical theology at the Iliff School of Theology, a United Methodist–related school of theology. Because the faculty of Iliff adopted a statement of full inclusion of GLBT students many years ago, a small but significant percentage of students at the school self-identify as gay, lesbian, bisexual, and transgendered. Many of these students were formed and experienced their call to ministry within the United Methodist tradition, which will not allow them to serve as clergy and be open about their sexual orientation. Thus, questions of whether to leave or to stay within the denomination are quite common at Iliff, as students struggle to adjudicate their sense of call and their loyalty to the community that formed them with the painful reality of what it would mean to serve in a denomination that does not recognize their identity and relationships fully.

Many students, as they realize the enormity of the challenges to their recognition as legitimate leaders presented by denominational structures, choose to leave the denomination of their formation for one that more fully recognizes them, commonly the United Church of Christ or the Unitarian Universalist Association. As Marilyn Alexander and James Preston describe this choice, it is both faithful and difficult: "Many gays/lesbians see moving out of their lifelong denominations as their only choice in order to be able to remember their baptism, re-experience God's grace and unconditional love, and have the equal standing called for in their baptism. To stay silently in a local church that does not actively challenge its general denomination's oppression of gays/lesbians is to die a silent death and contribute to the lies. To leave takes commitment to a faith in things that are not seen."[1]

The choice to leave allows the possibility of ordination while publically affirming one's orientation. However, such a choice does not remove one from the heterosexism and struggle that are still a part of these denominations that have moved toward fuller inclusion in clergy status. As our students sometimes note, the congregational-based polity of some of these denominations allow for being "ordained to unemployment," an experience many openly gay and lesbian clergy discover when they have switched to denominations that have a call-based system of clergy employment. Similar experiences occurred with women in the early years of the Lutheran Church of America (now ELCA) and the Presbyterian Church (USA) when they allowed for the ordination of women by law but through local practice often made it hard for women clergy to receive a call within the denomination.

Often in these student conversations about the ethics of staying within or leaving one's denomination, the choice to stay and to not be fully open

---

1. Alexander and Preston, *We Were Baptized*, 98–99.

about one's orientation is labeled as the choice to stay "closeted" in order to be ordained. Within GLBT communities, the metaphor of "coming out of the closet" has been closely associated with political activity towards full inclusion and equal rights in society for GLBT persons. As Elizabeth Stuart notes, "The act of 'coming out' became the ritual by which men and women claimed with pride an identity which others despised and in the process challenged and undermined the modern construction of the homosexual."[2] In this context, the choice to stay within the denomination becomes equated with hiding oneself, and at least implicit admission of the shameful nature of one's sexual orientation. For students who are out and proud within most contexts of their lives, and have been so for many years, the idea of choosing a professional context where one must remain closeted, even in part, is distasteful and inconceivable.

Additionally, the denominational strictures against ordination of GLBT persons raises the possibility that one's staying would signal a lack of integrity, a violation of the agreed-upon rules of the denomination. Staying requires going through the ordination process without being fully disclosive of an important part of one's self, despite the fact that, for many GLBT persons, their experience of their sexual orientation has played an important part of their faith journey and ongoing witness to God's presence and love. They fear that this decision results not only in a lack of integrity to the very structures one is making covenant within, but ongoing personal pain and frustration as they live within the institution. Even in the historically mainline Protestant congregations that declare themselves "reconciling" or "more light," congregants and leadership struggle with the embedded heterosexism of the culture, and often fail to live into a radically embracing community in subtle ways. Alexander and Preston describe this situation: "A life-quenching cycle often develops as gays/lesbians come into their personal power; as gays/lesbians come out more and more, they become less and less acceptable in mainline churches."[3] When combined with the inability to be fully upfront about one's reality within larger denominational structures, this experience can lead to personal pain and frustration heaped onto the already demanding clergy role.

Even given these daunting realities of the calling of GLBT persons to serve as clergy, I will argue that the decision to serve as clergy within

---

2. Stuart, *Gay and Lesbian*, 7.

3. Alexander and Preston, *We Were Baptized*, 105.

a denomination that does not fully recognize one's legitimacy could also be understood as a leadership practice contributing to the transformation of the institution and to full embrace of GLBT persons in the broader culture. Indeed, I will argue that the courage of individuals leading in this capacity are necessary for the transformation of the denomination by drawing on historical comparison with the movement towards full inclusion of women in ordained ministry in the United Methodist tradition. Given the limitations imposed by the structural inequality within the system, the choice to stay and serve without fully disclosing in all venues one's sexual orientation can be understood as a form of moral agency and activism rather than a form of hiding equated with being "closeted." In arguing that the choice to stay and be ordained within a denomination that does not recognize the legitimacy of one's being can be understood as a courageous political practice for change, I do not deny that the same actions could also be a choice to avoid activism. Nor do I intend to indicate that leaving the denomination of one's formation for a denomination that recognizes GLBT persons in clergy roles is an unfaithful choice. Rather, my hope is to articulate that both choices, leaving and staying, can be understood as agential leadership choices for persons whose calling from God is unjustly declared illegitimate by denominational structures.

Instead of utilizing the metaphor of "the closet" to label the practice of being ordained as a GLBT person in a denomination that does not sanction such a practice, the metaphor of "drag" as elaborated by philosopher Judith Butler is more appropriate. In her book *Gender Trouble,* Butler explores drag as a transgressive practice of gender performance that contributes to the destabilization of gender categories in the broader discourse. Although Butler denies that drag is an example of subversion or a model for political agency, she indicates that the practice calls into question the "naturalized knowledge" of gender categories with the potential contribution to a project of broader social change.[4] Butler notes the following: "When such categories come into question, the *reality* of gender is also put into crisis: it becomes unclear how to distinguish the real from the unreal. And this is the occasion in which we come to understand that what we take to be 'real,' what we invoke as the naturalized knowledge of gender is, in fact, a changeable and revisable reality."[5]

4. Butler, *Gender Trouble,* xxii.
5. Ibid., 23.

In other words, when individuals perform their gender identity in ways that call into question the certainty of their labeling as a "male" or "female" through the practice of drag, they potentially (though not necessarily) draw attention to the nature of gender as construction rather than a given, fixed reality. While Butler is quick to point out that such a practice "does not in itself constitute a political revolution," she notes that it potentially shifts people's ideas of what is real and what is possible. Sometimes, this lived practice of subverting gender precedes explicit thinking about the category and how it functions. Indeed, for Butler the subsequent change in thinking about gender could not happen without the experience generated by the practice of transgressive gender performance.[6] By refusing to produce and reproduce dominant narratives of gender that naturalize the category in the collective understanding of a culture and by exposing the nature of gender as a constructed reality, drag performances potentially contribute to the revolutionary project of denaturalizing the binary construction of gender.

When I describe the ordination of GLBT persons in a denomination that does not formally recognize the validity of their ordination as drag, I do not mean that persons literally are cross-dressing or engaging in gender ambiguous performance. Rather, I am using the metaphor of drag that Butler elaborated to explain a different but related experience. When the pastor I invoked at the beginning of this article presides over communion as an out lesbian minister in a local United Methodist congregation, she performs an identity that is a cultural impossibility. The legal restraints generated by the larger denominational body indicate that she cannot be a valid Christian leader and be involved in a committed same-sex relationship. Yet, for the members of this congregation, many of whom would initially have been reluctant to advocate for the ordination of GLBT persons, her pastoral identity becomes possible through the performance of it. As Butler notes, gender is "performative" because it "constitutes the identity it is purported to be."[7] While theoretically the members of the congregation might not understand themselves to be supporters of ordination of gay and lesbian persons, they have come to recognize the validity of such an identity because their pastor performed it prior to its being declared possible by the denomination.

6. Ibid., xxxiii.

7. Ibid., 33.

Performing the role before it is declared legitimate potentially leads to the cultural intelligibility of something that would otherwise be understood as confusing, illegitimate, or just plain wrong. Such a performance of an identity named impossible by the cultural structures is precisely what Butler is referring to when she talks about "drag" in the realm of gender performance. Drag performances ". . . swerve from their original purposes and inadvertently mobilize possibilities of 'subjects' that do not merely exceed the bounds of cultural intelligibility, but effectively expand the boundaries of what is, in fact, culturally intelligible."[8] Performing an identity that is culturally unintelligible calls into question the structures that deem it impossible, and thus begin the process of changing those structures and allowing for a different reality. In this way, such "drag" performances play an important role in bringing about social change within institutions and the broader culture.

## Drag and the Fight for Women's Ordination

While using the metaphor of drag to describe this leadership strategy for social change originates in contemporary queer theory, the strategy existed long before it was given such a name. Similar unintelligible performances of clergy identity by women were critical to the eventual legitimation of women's ordination in many denominations. Long before women had the legal right to serve as clergy in these denominations, they were serving as ministers within them. While I am using examples from the Methodist tradition in which I participate, similar examples could be given from other denominational traditions.

In the early years of the Methodist movement, women led class and prayer meetings and effectively ministered to the souls of their hearers. Even given what founder of the movement John Wesley understood to be the biblically grounded prohibition to women's preaching, he did not want to waste the talents of these women. Historian Carolyn DeSwarte Gifford describes his pragmatist response to the situation: "He advised the women to explain to their listeners that although Methodists did not allow women preachers, it was permissible for women to tell what was in their hearts concerning their faith."[9] Wesley invited women to continue to

---

8. Ibid., 39.
9. DeSwarte Gifford, "Introduction," not paginated.

speak publically about their faith and to expound the Scriptures even as they did not have the theological and cultural legitimacy to do so. Frances Willard, an advocate of women's ordination in the United States in the late 1800s, noted that John Wesley used "covert satire" when he did not forbid such women preachers but rather invited them to be discreet in his letter of January 31, 1791: "But conscience will not permit you to be silent when God commands you to speak. Yet I would have you give as little offence as possible; and, therefore, I would advise you not to speak at any place where a preacher is speaking at the same time, lest you should draw away his hearers."[10] With his joke about not competing with male preachers so as to not steal their listeners, Wesley affirms the strong capability of women speakers, and finds a way for them to serve even as he cannot yet recognize the category of woman preacher as legitimate. In other words, he invites drag performances from women ministers.

In addition to highlighting Wesley's recognition of women speakers, Frances Willard includes testimony of women preachers, some of whom had already been preaching in the Methodist church for as many as 15 years without official authority to do so at the time of her book's publication in 1889. Many of these women simply took up the work, understanding their role to be as "illustration" and "example" rather than making a public defense of women in ministry.[11] One of these unnamed clergywomen notes: "I am not given to argument on this question, believing in works much more than words. As a question in ethics, I see no controversy. It is surely right for a messenger to give a message of truth."[12] As Willard's text indicates, more than seventy years prior to receiving the legal authority to do so, women were performing the role of clergy in the Methodist church. Willard culminates her stirring defense of women serving as clergy by elaborating the ongoing work of women ministers without the authority of ordination in her own organization: "The National Woman's Christian Temperance Union has a department of evangelistic work, of Bible Readings, of Gospel Work for railroad employees, for soldiers, sailors, and lumbermen; of prison, jail, and police-station work; each of these departments being in charge of a woman . . . These make an aggregate of several thousands of women who are regularly studying and expounding

10. Willard, *Women in the Pulpit*, 111.

11. Ibid., 95.

12. Ibid., 96.

God's Word to the multitude, to say nothing of the army in home and foreign missionary work, and who are engaged in church evangelism."[13]

She goes on to note that they should take authority into their own hands, advising that they "knock only once more at the doors of the Methodist General Conference, and if their signals and entreaties are again uncivilly disregarded they should never knock again," instead choosing to ordain one another in order to serve the church of Christ.[14] Willard goes on to predict that if such a step was taken, the women would be surprised by the number of noble Wesleyan clergymen who would help out at their ordination service. Willard's text gives evidence that women had already been performing the role of clergy for some time, allowing many people to have the experience of the possibility of this previously "unintelligible" identity.

Before moving on to the experience of clergywomen as initially unintelligible even after their role was legitimated in the denomination, I want to emphasize that serving as clergy prior to being culturally intelligible is not an easy role to fulfill. Willard's careful historical and theological work in her book, and that of many other women in multiple books about the legitimacy of women's ordination written in the century after, poignantly indicate years of theological and biblical searching to justify the legitimacy of women in this calling. Her well-worded defenses point to the ongoing attacks on the authority and being of these women, requiring the kind of "bulletproof" faith that Candace Chellew-Hodge has advocated for contemporary GLBT Christians who go public with their identity.[15] Drag performances incite resistance, sometimes even violent resistance. To publically perform a culturally unintelligible identity risks sanction and mockery. Frances Willard withheld the names of the women she quoted in her text for good reason; they ran the risk of being harmed if they were "outed" as ministers.

One of the women willing to be named in Willard's book was Catharine Booth, Joint-Chief of the Salvation Army at the time, who noted that the primary objection against women preaching in public was that such a performance was "unnatural and unfeminine." Like Butler, she goes on to indicate that such an understanding makes the mistake of

13. Ibid., 57.
14. Ibid., 172.
15. Chellew-Hodge, *Bulletproof Faith*.

"confounding nature with custom": "Use or custom makes things appear to us natural which, in reality, are very unnatural; while, on the other hand novelty and rarity make very natural things appear strange and contrary to nature . . . Making allowance for the novelty of the thing, we cannot discover anything either unnatural or immodest in a Christian woman, becomingly attired, appearing on a platform or in a pulpit."[16] For Booth, the problem with women serving as clergy is not that such a role defies nature or modesty, but rather that it was a novelty in a culture that did not regularly allow for the public leadership of women. People were not yet accustomed to seeing women as clergy, and thus they found their performance in the role strange.

Remarkably, despite the ongoing struggle of women towards full equality in society over the following century, woman ordained in the first few decades after being given the legal legitimacy to do so by the denomination continued to find that their performance of the clergy role was initially unintelligible to both congregants and people in the broader culture. In a 1988 survey of attitudes toward women in the ordained ministry in the United Methodist Church, more than thirty years after the first women were ordained by the denomination, clergy women still discuss the reality that people are unaccustomed to seeing a woman pastor: "As a clergywoman, I know that when I am appointed to a new congregation, I face a mixed reception, but this is primarily because people are not used to seeing a woman in the role of pastor. So I just do my work and let people discover that I am indeed a minister—with individual strengths and weaknesses, just like any clergyman. Reactions to me have been overwhelmingly positive."[17] This single statement by one respondent bears out in the trends of the study. People who had experience with a clergywoman as pastor were both willing to accept another one as their leader and generally had a positive attitude about women in ministry.[18] Without such experience, they were more likely to reject women ministers as potential leaders in their congregation. This means that women entering a congregation as a leader often entered a situation in which they were initially granted little role-related legitimacy and authority, despite the fact that they now had legal legitimacy within the denomination. However,

16. Willard, *Women in the Pulpit*, 104.

17. United Methodist Church (US), *Survey*, 20.

18. Ibid., 1.

as the women performed the role without authority, they expanded the possibility of the role of pastor extending to women and created cultural intelligibility and authority where previously there was none.

The experience of the first generation of women in the clergy role with the full authority of the institution behind them bears out the importance of engaging in drag performances until they are culturally recognizable. Until they have had the experience of interacting with a clergywoman, many people are not sure what to make of a woman in this role. Lutheran clergywoman Mary Ann Moller-Gunderson relates her experience of wearing a clerical collar to the grocery store: "A complete stranger approached me and asked, 'What are you?' The lack of female clergy as role models, the absence of biblical and theological teaching tools, and the newness of women clergy all required a period of living into our decision to ordain women."[19] Moller-Gunderson's anecdote and analysis describes how a person experiencing a woman in clergy dress for the first time literally could not recognize her. Confused by the presentation of a woman in what is supposed to be a man's role, the person in the grocery store found the performance unintelligible. Moller-Gunderson expresses the need to live into this new reality before people can fully understand and appreciate it, combining educational efforts with lived experience to move from drag to full intelligibility.

Drag performances such as women in clergy garb, or GLBT persons serving in denominations that do not recognize their legitimacy, can be deeply unsettling to persons who have never encountered them. Karen Armstrong talks about the "profound unease" that people in the Church of England experienced when they imagined women at the altar prior to the practice of ordination of women. She argued, "The Church should try to help people overcome this instinctive revulsion by getting them used to the idea gradually."[20] "Instinctive revulsion" is strong language, but the phrase captures the embodied and unthinking reaction generated by a dominant culture embedded in social histories of inequality that has trained persons to recognize certain role performances and to reject others. Armstrong notes that the challenge presented by such an image reaches beyond encountering a cultural oddity to truly challenge the very foundations of self and identity of persons: "As the debate about women

19. Moller-Gunderson, "Persistent Voices," 126.
20. Armstrong, *The End of Silence*, 195.

priests progressed, people would often speak of their whole faith, their entire world view being radically undermined by the idea."[21] Given the deep and embodied formation, incremental movement towards recognition and legitimacy requires the careful laying of groundwork through encounters with people performing the role. Patience Purchas attributes the success of newly ordained women priests in the Church of England to "the groundwork done in previous years." She describes an effort called "Your next vicar could be a woman" in which one Board of Ministry invited women already serving as deacons to preach throughout the diocese. This experience led to greater understanding and acceptance: "The fear of the unknown or novel was overcome and frequently the women had the experience of being told something like 'I thought I wouldn't like seeing a woman preaching, leading worship/taking a funeral, but it was all right.'"[22] Again, what was anticipated as deeply unsettling or revolting became possible in the actual experience of it.

Similar to the long process of women gaining recognition and legitimacy in the role of clergy, GLBT persons working for this authority in the church may gain it by serving in the role prior to their official recognition. Like the experiences of women clergy, congregants will likely only come to feel comfortable and even excited about the gifts of GLBT clergy through experiences with GLBT clergy. Much like how the struggle for women to receive full clergy rights within denominations took place in structures populated primarily by men, the process of granting legal authority for ordination within the denominations that do not yet allow for the ordination of GLBT persons occurs in structures dominated by straight clergy and lay delegates. In order for such persons to become comfortable with the idea of GLBT clergy, they will need experiences of being in ministry with GLBT persons. Such experience is impossible without drag performances, persons willing to take on the role before they have cultural intelligibility and legal authority to do so.

But is getting ordained when one does not technically have the denominational authority to do so ethical? Georgia Harkness described the need for women to become ordained on principle in order to bring about social change in the church. While she argued that "ordination ought to be an authentic personal commitment, not simply an instrument of social

21. Ibid., 195–96.
22. Purchas, "From Expectations to Realities," 126.

change," she also recognized that such an action witnessed to "the possibility of equal status for women" and that she believed "this step might give some encouragement and perhaps help to open opportunities to women courageously serving small rural parishes as approved supplies."[23] Harkness was ordained prior to the official denominational actions that would allow her full annual conference membership in 1956. She recognized that being ordained before she had the full authority to do so helped bring about social change and therefore was a principled decision to work for justice: "The ordination of concerned and prepared women helps to challenge the present barriers of conservatism in the churches, and perhaps indirectly in other spheres. This would justify it when it is done seriously as a matter of principle, even if no question of expediency were involved."[24] While GLBT persons who face the decision whether or not to pursue ordination prior to full denominational recognition must have the final say about whether their personal sense of integrity and calling leads to such action, to foreclose the possibility of ordination entirely on the basis of contested covenantal rules seems unduly constricted ethical reasoning that does not take into account the exclusionary nature of existing structures and the limitations they generate on the agency of individuals who are called to ministry.

## But I Don't Want to Be an Activist!

One of the struggles for GLBT persons entering the clergy, and for that matter GLBT persons getting married and parenting and engaging any number of other life practices, is that they cannot engage in such practices "innocently" or apolitically. A same-sex couple holding hands in the park can be perceived as an act of activism even when the intention is merely to show affections to one's beloved. Because of the heterosexism of the broader culture, everything from talking about one's orientation to getting ordained becomes understood as an explicitly political act rather than merely a faithful act of following one's calling. Of course, ordination is a political act for straight persons as well, but the privilege of being part of the dominant culture is that they do not have to perceive it as such. While many straight allies are beginning to realize that getting married in

---

23. Harkness, *Women in Church*, 214–15.
24. Ibid., 215.

states that do not allow same-sex couples to marry and getting ordained in denominations that do not allow persons engaged in public same-sex relationships to be ordained are political acts that reproduce the dominant culture, their political involvement in the process of reproducing discriminatory policies is not often highlighted. Systems of privilege are sustained in this way: by declaring one status or identity "normal" and affording it rights that are denied persons from other identity categories.

Similar to how parishioners objected to women preachers in the church prior to women's ordination becoming legally possible in mainline denominations and experiencing them in the role of clergy, many parishioners find the idea of GLBT pastors objectionable because they have never experienced such leadership. By serving as clergy in traditions that do not legally allow for such service, GLBT persons are making possible an identity that is deemed unintelligible by denominational structures and by individuals in local congregations. Given recent removal of restrictions against the ordination of GLBT persons in many denominations, I hope that GLBT clergy persons are not forced to wait for 80 years like Willard and her colleagues before they are formally recognized by the legal structures. To continue to serve without being able to be fully disclosive of who they are robs the church of the full measure of the Spirit's gifts being poured out through GLBT persons in the fullness of their identity and sexuality. However, in this time in which some denominations are struggling towards justice and full recognition of God's calling to all persons, I do want to recognize that deciding to stay within these denominations and to serve does not have to mean being closeted, in the sense that this metaphor has been used within the GLBT community. To claim the practice of drag as a political practice of exposing the constructed limitations of our current understandings of who can and cannot serve as clergy allows for a different understanding of those who stay within the denomination and become ordained. Exposing these limitations is an act of leadership rather than an act of hiding. This replicates the history of the movement towards full recognition of women within the church, and the cultural and institutional change that happened alongside this movement. Such change is agonizingly slow, as women clergy who continue to lag behind in appointments to large and vital churches, salaries, and even recognition of their legitimacy, particularly in strongholds of the denomination, can attest. However, to add the further burden of being labeled "in the closet" while engaging in the very practices that will potentially lead to recognition of GLBT clergy as culturally intelligible makes such leadership even more difficult.

# BIBLIOGRAPHY

Alexander, Marilyn Bennet, and James Preston. *We Were Baptized Too: Claiming God's Grace for Lesbians and Gays*. Louisville: Westminster John Knox, 1996.

Armstrong, Karen. *The End of Silence: Women and Priesthood*. London: Fourth Estate, 1993.

Butler, Judith. *Gender Trouble: Feminism and the Subversion of Identity*. Tenth Anniversary Edition. London: Routledge, 1999.

Chellew-Hodge, Candace. *Bulletproof Faith: A Spiritual Survival Guide for Gay and Lesbian Christians*. San Francisco: Jossey-Bass, 2008.

Gifford, Carolyn DeSwarte. "Introduction." In *The Defense of Women's Rights to Ordination in the Methodist Episcopal Church*. New York: Garland, 1987.

Harkness, Georgia. *Women in Church and Society: A Historical and Theological Inquiry*. Nashville: Abingdon, 1972.

Moller-Gunderson, Mary Ann. "Persistent Voices Champion the Inclusion of Women." In *Lutheran Women in Ordained Ministry, 1970–1995: Reflections and Perspectives*, edited by Gloria E. Bengtson, 123–28. Minneapolis: Augsburg, 1995.

Purchas, Patience. "From Expectations to Realities: and the Future." In *Women Priests: The First Years*, edited by Hilary Wakeman, 117–35. London: Dartman, Longman & Todd, 1996.

Stuart, Elizabeth. *Gay and Lesbian Theologies: Repetitions with Critical Difference*. Burlington, VT: Ashgate, 2003.

United Methodist Church (US). General Council on Ministries. Office of Research. *Survey of United Methodist Opinion: Attitudes toward Women in the Ordained Ministry*. Susan Swan Mura, principal researcher. Dayton: General Council on Ministries, 1988.

Willard, Frances E. *Women in the Pulpit*. Chicago: Woman's Temperance Publication Association, 1889. Reprinted as: *The Defense of Women's Rights to Ordination in the Methodist Episcopal Church*. Edited by Carolyn DeSwarte Gifford. New York: Garland, 1987.

# Pastoral Response

## Dan Geslin

IN THE INTEREST OF full disclosure, I am an actual LGBTQ person who has served as an openly gay ordained pastor for twenty-five years in the United Church of Christ (UCC). I currently serve Sixth Avenue UCC in Denver, a congregation that openly welcomes and affirms LGBTQ students from Iliff as interns, and hosts many LGBTQ refugees from the United Methodist Church (UMC). I was once such a refugee myself, leaving the Lutheran church of my formation midway through seminary to transfer into the UCC all those years ago.

As Dr. Turpin has observed, leaving the church of one's formation is painful, disorienting, and sometimes faith killing, especially for one who feels called and committed to ministry within one's denomination. It was for me. It was the only time in my life that I considered suicide. For when one leaves the denomination of one's childhood, one is not just leaving an institution, but the community of one's memories and identity, family and friends, faith and schooling. So my first practical, pastoral reflection on Dr. Turpin's essay is the grave responsibility that UMC teachers, ministers, and congregations have in relation to all of their queer members and their families and friends, but especially to those who feel called to ordained ministry. This is a life and death matter.

I sympathize with Dr. Turpin's loyalty to the United Methodist Church as the motivation pulsing beneath the surface of her essay. Such loyalty to a denomination is something I once felt for the Evangelical Lutheran Church in America (ELCA)—indeed, without such loyalty there would be no conflict in the hearts of LGBTQ seminarians who are asked to sacrifice our happiness, integrity, and peace of mind on the altar of denominationalism. Yet one of the unforeseen and deep blessings that I experienced when I moved from one denomination to another was that it freed me to be more fully and simply *Christian*. In seminary I had come to put my faith in my denomination to ordain me, so letting go of that old vine, like Jane swinging through the jungle in midair before firmly grasping a new vine, was when I truly put my faith in G_d. I have a deep and abiding love for the UCC, which gave me a home when I was abandoned by the church of my baptism, but that love is not the same as the loyalty bred into one by the church of one's origin. I think my experience makes me a better minister—a better evangelist, preacher, and pastoral counselor to seekers.

Therefore my second practical, pastoral reflection is to beg UMC teachers and ministers to let God's queer people go, if we need to, in order to fulfill our call to the ordained ministry not of the UMC but of Jesus Christ. When I made my transition, my mentor, the Reverend Dr. Wally Stuhr, then president of the Pacific Lutheran Theological Seminary, after trying to get me to stay Lutheran by staying in the closet, knew when it was time to faithfully say, "I hate to see you go, Dan, but you have a call and it can only be answered elsewhere." We remain friends to this day, in part because he put his energy as a straight ally not into trying to control me but into working to change the denomination's policy that excluded me.

That brings me to my third practical, pastoral reflection, which is in support of Dr. Turpin's thesis. In the summer of 2010 I attended the official ELCA worship service in San Francisco celebrating that denomination's vote for the full inclusion of otherwise qualified queer candidates to the ordained ministry, and welcoming back previously ordained LGBT clergy who had been thrown out on the basis of the old policy. It was a deeply moving worship service for all. But because it was held at the church where I had done my seminary fieldwork many years before, it was especially moving for me as I came full circle and felt closure within God's embrace. Although I could not possibly have done it myself, I felt grateful to the queer people who had stayed in the ELCA, ministering from within the closet and working for change with the help of ever more nongay allies. The personal costs that they suffered are immense, and I would *never* tell another LGBT or Q person that she or he should martyr their integrity for the cause of denominationalism. But just as I was called to ministry through changing denominations, I honor the truth that some queers are called to a ministry of staying within—what has long been called in our movement, "subverting by staying in place." But that takes an enormous toll on one's emotional, psychological, and spiritual health and well-being. So, yes, that can be an honorable call if it is authentic. If it is not authentic, it will lead to disaster.

Personally, I see no need to stretch the loaded metaphor of drag to fit the question before us, which is how lesbian, gay, bisexual, and transgender seminarians should respond to the fact that the United Methodist Church officially and categorically sees us as too sinful and unclean to be authorized ministers . . . if we are honest about who we are. I think what Dr. Turpin is suggesting is what we in the LGBT community have long called "passing," a term borrowed from the African American community and referring to light-skinned blacks who transgressed the color line in segregated societies. As Judith Butler herself attests, drag includes an element of parody from the outside. But passing inside raises ethical issues more fitting, I think, to this ecclesiastical context. What is the responsibility of the lesbian or gay man who can outwardly pass the UMC's requirement of heteronormativity not only to oneself and one's career advancement, but to the community of one's true identity, as well as to the policies of the denomination? Forgive my simplicity, but these are my two practical, pastoral questions. What does God call us to in life and in ministry if not human health and wholeness within the unconditional love and grace of Jesus Christ? And how can I offer that to others in a denomination that will not offer it to me?

As someone who has worked these past 25 years doing the daily, practical, pastoral work of preaching and teaching, counseling and companioning the distraught and the dying, baptizing those newly born into the faith and serving communion to the faithful and the searching—not to mention refereeing congregational fights and advocating for social justice—I do not believe that denominational loyalty can sustain one's spirit or comfort one's soul in the work of ordained ministry which, by its very nature, is not just a call to a job, but a call to give one's whole self. I know some people do it—usually with the help of private therapy and a secret circle of friends—and such people merit respect for the choice that they make to serve under such agonizing circumstances. But it requires a personal relationship with the G_d of the burning bush who is beyond all names, denominations, doctrines, and dogmas.

I have sympathy for Dr. Turpin as she watches UMC students leave. I also have sympathy for the UMC seminarians who regularly come to Sixth Avenue UCC. I sit with them as they grieve the loss of the denomination that formed them, but now excludes them, if they're honest. Now that UCCers, Episcopalians, Lutherans, and Presbyterians all ordain otherwise qualified LGBTQ candidates, the United Methodist Church is being left behind by our mainline ecumenical family for officially excluding "self-avowed practicing homosexuals."[1] Along with many others who live in the Good News of Jesus Christ, I pray for the day when "open hearts, open minds, open doors" is not just a PR slogan but the gospel truth.

## BIBLIOGRAPHY

United Methodist Church (US). *The Book of Discipline of the United Methodist Church*. Nashville: United Methodist Publishing House, 2008.

---

1. United Methodist Church (U.S.) *The Book of Discipline*, article 4, ¶ 304.3.

# Chapter Six

## Leading with Grace
### *Authentic Leadership in the Church*

### Melanie Rosa

### A Stained-Glass Ceiling

RALPH WAS A PLEASANT seventy-five-year-old man who faithfully supported his church. I had only been his pastor for six months, and liked him very much. He was in church every Sunday and always gracious. One Sunday after worship he waited to shake my hand and said, "Sweetheart, you are a good preacher. But you would be a great preacher ... if only you were a man." I knew he was kidding, but I also knew that for Ralph and others, these words contained elements of truth. I have been an ordained United Methodist minister serving in a variety of churches for twenty-five years, always as the first female pastor in congregations large and small, rural and urban. In every setting I have initially encountered skepticism and reservation, primarily because of my gender. Of course, one must be careful about raising the gender issue too often, but we are remiss if we fail to raise it at all. Gender continues to profoundly shape perceptions about leadership, capability, and effectiveness.

There is a crisis in pastoral leadership today, as reflected in the mountains of statistics about membership decline, ineffective clergy, financial shortfalls, and institutional pain. Additionally, there are clergy shortages in many of the major Christian and Jewish denominations, and there is growing concern about clergy quality and competence. And yet, the issue of gender is largely absent from most of these discussions. This is remarkable, in light of the fact that "most sociologists and theological educators agree that women's entry into the ordained ministry represents the most significant transformation in pastoral leadership . . . since the Reformation."[1]

Clergywomen in most major mainline denominations still face more obstacles and difficulties than their male counterparts. Since 1993 the Anna Howard Shaw Center at the Boston University School of Theology has been conducting a retention study of United Methodist clergywomen. Year after year this study reveals that "women are leaving local church ministry at a much higher rate than male clergy." In their efforts to understand the reasons behind this phenomenon, the researchers concluded: "They leave the local church primarily due to lack of support from the hierarchical system, difficulty maintaining their integrity in the current system, family responsibilities, and rejection from their congregations."[2] The most painful accounts contained in this report were the personal stories of women who were mistreated by congregations that cut their salaries, who were subjected to wildly unrealistic expectations, whose clergy colleagues considered them "little helpers," and whose bishops and superintendents misrepresented congregations and the women themselves.[3] There were accounts of women who were told that their participation on the youth ski trip would count as vacation time, and whose personal and family lives were mercilessly scrutinized by parishioners. Within the United Methodist Church, very few women are currently serving in large membership churches (over 1,000 members). While 23 percent of clergy within the denomination are female (14 percent are ordained elders), less than 6 percent of the total number of clergywomen serve large membership churches. This is a stained glass ceiling which has been very difficult to crack. Salary studies in various annual conferences

1. McDougall, "Weaving Garments of Grace," 151.

2. Shaw Center, *United Methodist Clergywomen Retention Study.* Online: http://www.bu.edu/shaw/publications/the-clergy-womens-retention-study/.

3. Ibid.

reveal that women consistently earn less than their male colleagues, even with equal years of service.

Consultant Carol Becker believes that religious denominations are by nature gendered organizations, with "sexuality and gender . . . deeply imbedded in the nature of the denominations as organizations." She concludes that both mainline and evangelical denominations themselves are "deeply anti-feminine and fundamentally masculine."[4] Becker's assessment would account for the ongoing obstacles women encounter, even after all these years, serving as spiritual leaders in the church.

## The Myth of Competence

This discouraging state of affairs does not diminish the fact that significant gains have been made in recent decades. As of 2006 women accounted for 34.4 percent of the enrollment at U.S. seminaries that accept female students. Currently female students outnumber men in United Methodist seminaries. Women have made deep and lasting contributions to the spiritual life of congregations, bringing unique and creative gifts to the local church and judicatory bodies. Yet there is still a very long way to go. Joy McDougall interviewed eight highly gifted female seminary students in 2003, and was stunned by their "self-doubts, ambivalence, and even guilt about their call to ordained ministry."[5] How can women called to Christian ministry lead with grace, trust, and confidence in the midst of a culture that frequently feels threatening and unwelcoming?

My ministerial career has been characterized by a sustained effort to adapt to the fundamentally masculine system that is the Christian church. I have worked hard to succeed within this system and to become more competent, capable and proficient. I have read the latest books, studied successful pastors and growing churches, and attended more seminars than I can remember. I believed that if I acquired just the right set of skills and techniques, everything would fall into place and the churches I served would flourish. I have tried to be strong, decisive, and visionary. I have deliberately exhibited the more traditional leadership qualities, so that my gender would not be an issue. I knew that according to some congregational surveys, lay people said that the qualities they most desired in clergy were competence, courage and authority. While trying to "lead like

4. Becker, *Leading Women*, 75.

5. McDougall, "Weaving Garments of Grace," 150.

a man" I felt it necessary to deny my vulnerability and creativity. I did not believe that the spiritual leadership which comes naturally to me would be valued or effective.

Professor and consultant Israel Galindo writes about the "myth of competence," which he defines as the exaggerated expectation of performance and successful results. He writes: "The myth of competence is the attitude, fed by chronic anxiety, that engenders the belief that personal self-worth, relevance, and meaning reside in *external* definitions and assurances of being competent in all that one does. It manifests itself in ways of functioning and relating in the church that can result in burnout and depression."[6] I have wholeheartedly accepted the myth of competence in all things, with the resulting sense of frustration and inadequacy.

Only in recent years have I come to understand the toll this has taken upon my spirit and psyche. In light of this realization, I have tried to redefine what success in ministry looks like, because producing positive results in every area of ministry (administration, management, supervision, fundraising, missions, evangelism, social justice, preaching, teaching, pastoral care, and mediating the presence of God to everyone, everywhere), is beyond impossible. Writes John Berntsen: "The leader is humbled by the very work of ministry: by not always having the answers, by lack of giftedness for important ministries . . . resentment toward 'problem' people, and by disillusionment with the once-held ideal of the church. James Barrie, the sentimental author of *Peter Pan*, said, 'Life is one long lesson in humility.' So, too, is the practice of ministry."[7] I have learned that a humble, genuine, and emotionally intelligent style of leadership has a liberating effect upon congregations, and interestingly enough, brings about positive results. I am increasingly drawn toward a model of authentic leadership that empowers and transforms, spiritual leadership grounded in God's grace.

## Toward a Model of Authentic Leadership

Authentic leadership can be explained in relation to its four characteristics: the leader as cultivator of an environment, the inner life of the leader, emotional sensitivity, and an experimental mindset.

6. Galindo, "The Myth of Competence," 148.
7. Berntsen, *Cross-Shaped Leadership*, 129.

## The Leader as Cultivator of an Environment

In their groundbreaking book *The Missional Leader,* Alan Roxburgh and Fred Romanuk offer just such a liberating model of church leadership, with the pastor as cultivator of an environment. They write: "missional church is not about new techniques or programs for the church. At its core, missional church is how we cultivate a congregational environment where God is the center of conversation and God shapes the focus and work of the people . . . it is about shaping cultural imagination within a congregation wherein people discern what God might be about among them and in their community."[8] These authors suggest that the dominant models of church leadership, pastoral (caring for the flock through visitation, counseling, and care) and entrepreneurial (taking charge, producing results and leading the church into the future), would be more effectively replaced with missional leadership, characterized by a leader "who is a *cultivator* of an environment that discerns God's activities among the congregation and in its context. It is leadership that cultivates the practice of indwelling Scripture and discovering places for experiment and risk as people discover that the Spirit of God's life-giving future in Jesus is among them."[9] This allows the transforming spirit of God to work through what is already in place: congregations, organizational systems, and leaders who are not trying to do everything themselves. Missional leadership seems uniquely suited to the collaborative and creative leadership style that comes naturally to many women.

## The Inner Life of the Leader

The inner life of the leader is of critical importance for transforming and effective leadership. In his book, *In the Name of Jesus: Reflections on Christian Leadership,* Henri Nouwen writes about two temptations for spiritual leaders: to be relevant and to be spectacular. These are seductive temptations for women eager to prove themselves, particularly when we are tempted to measure our effectiveness by growth in finances and membership. Nouwen writes, "I am deeply convinced that the Christian leader of the future is called to be completely irrelevant and to stand in this world with nothing to offer but his or her own vulnerable self. That is the way Jesus came to reveal God's love . . . a God who loves us not because of

8. Roxburgh and Romanuk, *The Missional Leader,* 26.
9. Roxburgh and Romanuk, *The Missional Leader,* 27.

what we do or accomplish."[10] Letting go of our need to perform, impress, and produce results is counterintuitive and difficult, but it allows God's plans and purposes to emerge. Ultimately, we have nothing more to offer those we lead than honestly sharing who we are and reminding them whose we are.

In a pamphlet titled *Leading from Within: Reflections on Spirituality and Leadership*, Parker Palmer writes of the necessity for leaders to go deep within themselves in order to lead with authenticity and power. He writes about honestly facing our own pain, demons, and fear in order to offer others a transparent and transforming presence. Palmer lists some of the seductive shadows for spiritual leaders: insecurity about our own worth; the perception that the universe is a hostile place; functional atheism; fear of failure; denial of death.

These shadows ring very true in my own experience and that of several of my clergy sisters. First, many clergywomen live with deep insecurity within the Christian church, worried that we can never completely represent a God viewed by the majority of people as male, and that our gifts and graces will not be appreciated. Second, the perception that the universe is a hostile place takes hold when one is subjected to excessive scrutiny and petty criticism. Third, the insidious attraction of the superwoman syndrome is the assumption that if only we work longer and harder, we will prove ourselves worthy. Palmer calls this "functional atheism" because we act as if fruitful ministry is entirely up to us, rather than trusting in God. Fourth, the fear of failure is always lurking, because some are expecting it, and if we fail to produce positive results in ministry, it must be related to our own shortcomings and deficiencies. The final shadow is the denial of death. Palmer suggests that we do not allow things to die in our culture or in the church. "Leaders everywhere demand that they themselves and the people who work for them artificially maintain things that are no longer alive. Projects and programs that should have been laid down ten years ago are still on the life support system."[11] To identify and acknowledge these inner shadows is a liberating step toward leading with authenticity, hope, and trust in God.

10. Nouwen, *In the Name of Jesus*, 17.
11. Palmer, *Leading from Within*, 32–37.

## Emotional Sensitivity

Leadership experts have only recently identified what many women have instinctively understood: the profound relationship between emotional sensitivity and effective leadership. In their book, *Primal Leadership: Realizing the Power of Emotional Intelligence,* Daniel Goleman, Annie McKee and Richard Boyatzis describe the difference emotional intelligence makes, arguing that "the best leaders have found effective ways to understand and improve the way they handle their own and other people's emotions. This emotional task of the leader is primal..in two senses: It is both the original and the most important act of leadership."[12] The authors list 18 competencies of emotional intelligence, including self-awareness, self-control, empathy, and relationship management. Most women are socialized to pay close attention to relationships and emotions, thus emotional intelligence is one of the best leadership qualities women bring to ministry.

Of course we must be careful about stereotyping female leadership and suggesting that women's natural gifts make them ideally suited for effective ministry. It is simplistic to believe that women are one way and men another, because individuals are unique and there are always exceptions. Women in leadership can be hierarchical and authoritarian, just as men can be collaborative and creative. Nevertheless, according to the research of church consultant Carol Becker[13] and others, women do have a distinctly different style of leadership from their male counterparts. Generally speaking, women are more process oriented, valuing the journey as much as the end result. They use participatory management more frequently in a collaborative effort to gather input before making decisions. Women exhibit a willingness to share information, and for the most part do not see themselves as experts with all the answers. Women exhibit a fundamental concern for human relationships and are quick to collaborate and negotiate. Women prefer win-win scenarios, with positive outcomes shared by the entire community. These attributes are desperately needed in a time when leaders of all institutions are suspect, and the church is desperately trying to engage new generations.

12. Goleman et al., *Primal Leadership,* 4–5.
13. Becker, *Leading Women,* 38–42.

## An Experimental Mindset

In his book *Leadership without Easy Answers,* Ronald Heifetz compiled a decade of research on leadership in anxious times. Through the study of politics, psychiatry, and various leaders throughout history, Heifetz concludes that effective leaders must be willing to upset and disrupt people, to constantly challenge equilibrium. He writes, "A leader risks challenging people, directly or indirectly, slow or fast, soft or hard, guided by a comprehension of and sensitivity to the changes people have to make in their lives."[14] Heifetz believes effective leaders must learn to adapt quickly, improvise, and trust chaos. "Leadership . . . requires an experimental mindset; the willingness to work by trial and error . . . no analysis or catalog can substitute for a leader's improvisational skills."[15] This is the future of leadership in our time, and many are already paving the way in the Christian church.

Adaptive spiritual leadership matters deeply in this world which cries out for hope, healing, and direction. There has never been a greater need for creative, visionary leadership which empowers and inspires others. For the Christian church to remain viable we must find new ways of calling, training, and supporting diverse leaders who are able to guide spiritual seekers through this challenging time into God's future. Christian leadership in the days ahead will, of necessity, be dramatically different from anything we have previously known. Traditional assumptions and methods have long been proven obsolete, and while people are spiritually hungry, they are highly suspicious of religious institutions.

Leadership for these times will no longer be about assuming a role or acquiring skill sets, it will be about the embodiment of certain qualities, including the ability to bring diverse people together in a common cause. "The leader of the future isn't a person. It is a team. It is a group of people gifted and called by God to lead. It is a community drawn together by a sense of the possible."[16] Effective spiritual leaders are change agents, cultivators of holy environments, those who thrive in chaos and embrace uncertainty. They are women and men who, with God's help, are called to unleash the possibility and potential in others while serving as living

14. Heifetz, *Leadership without Easy Answers,* 243.
15. Ibid., 242.
16. Jones, "Leading for the Future," 177–78.

reminders of that one who continually invites all of us to participate in the creation of a new reality.

## Foremothers in Authentic Leadership

I am grateful for those who have pioneered authentic leadership and helped to pave the way for those who came after them in the church. Their risks, struggles and sacrifices have made my ministry possible. Two such pioneers come to mind. Margaret Scheve was the very first woman ordained in the Rocky Mountain Conference of the Methodist Church. She graduated from the Iliff School of Theology in 1934, but was not ordained an elder until eighteen years later; she was finally admitted to clergy membership, on trial, in 1956. No congregation would accept a woman pastor in those days, so Rev. Scheve worked for twenty years as the secretary to the bishop of the conference. She was appointed to her first church in 1973, almost forty years after graduation from seminary, and twenty years after ordination. Her endless patience finally paid off, and she served churches with great effectiveness before retiring from active ministry. Rev. Scheve was never bitter about waiting so long to serve as a pastor, rather she was one of the most gracious and spirit-filled spiritual leaders I have ever known. She mentored many women and rejoiced to know that she helped to make the path easier for those women who followed her into ministry in the local church.

Grace Huck was the second woman to receive full clergy rights in the Methodist church. She was also admitted in 1956, after being ordained elder in 1949. "While a child, Huck had practiced preaching to cattle and sheep on her father's ranch."[17] A true pioneer, she served churches for sixty-five years in rural North Dakota. She endured suspicion, slander, and overt discrimination throughout her career. In 2006, when she was ninety years old, she addressed more than 1,500 clergywomen at the International Clergywomen's Consultation in Chicago. She told those gathered that she was able to keep a positive attitude during sixty-five years in ministry by keeping her focus upon the radical values of Jesus. She remembered her call, and never forgot that the God who called her to ministry would not abandon her.[18] This diminutive woman undoubtedly

17. Schmidt, *Grace Sufficient*, 283.
18. Huck, "Rules for Walking on Water."

endured more setbacks and heartaches than most of us could imagine, and yet she was deeply grounded in a faith that allowed her to remain true to herself. She did not simply survive sixty-five years of active ministry; she flourished, and blessed countless lives in the process.

These women modeled a positive, spirit-filled style of authentic leadership, as they continued to trust in the God who called them to ministry, without giving in to frustration or bitterness. Such examples of positive perseverance are important for women who still encounter suspicion and resistance when leading in the church. Those who have gone before us serve as reminders that attitude and fortitude work wonders, even in a deeply entrenched patriarchal system. They also remind us that such systems are always in need of liberation and transformation.

## Postscript

About five years ago I was asked to officiate at Ralph's funeral. While meeting with his wife and daughter to plan the service I learned that over the years I had become his ". . . all time favorite pastor." These women shared with me Ralph's deep reservations when I was first appointed to the church, and that he considered leaving. Yet over time he gradually warmed to me, and came to appreciate my unique style of ministry. His family said that he grew closer to God than he had ever been, due in part to my spiritual leadership. It was gratifying to discover that God had used me to bless a man who was initially disappointed to have me as his pastor. These days I keep Ralph in my heart as I serve in a very different kind of ministry. As a district superintendent, I support and supervise forty different churches made up of ranchers, farmers, retirees, executives and Fortune 500 CEOs. Even though I know that some of the people I meet (men and women alike) continue to believe that a female pastor is less competent, less capable, and less effective than a man, it does not bother me nearly as much. My goal is to remain faithful to the God who has called me to authentic spiritual leadership in the church.

## BIBLIOGRAPHY

Anna Howard Shaw Center. 1999 *United Methodist Clergywoman Retention Study*. Boston: Boston University School of Theology, 1993–2010. Online: http://www.bu.edu/shaw/publications/the-clergy-womens-retention-study/.

Becker, Carol. *Leading Women*. Nashville: Abingdon, 1996.

Berntsen, John A. *Cross-Shaped Leadership: On the Rough and Tumble of Parish Practice*. Herndon, VA: Alban Institute, 2008.

Galindo, Israel. "The Myth of Competence." In *Leadership in Congregations*, edited by Richard Bass, 147–53. Harvesting the Learnings. Herndon, VA: Alban Institute, 2007.

Goleman, Daniel et al. *Primal Leadership: Realizing the Power of Emotional Intelligence*. Boston: Harvard Business School Press, 2002.

Heifetz, Ronald. *Leadership Without Easy Answers*. Cambridge, MA: Belknap, 1998.

Huck, Grace. "Rules for Walking on Water." Sermon preached at the 2006 International Clergywomen's Consultation, Chicago, Illinois, August 13–17, 2006.

Jones, Jeffrey D. "Leading for the Future." In *Leadership in Congregations*, edited by Richard Bass, 173–79. Harvesting the Learnings. Herndon, VA: Alban Institute, 2007.

McDougall, Joy. "Weaving Garments of Grace: En-gendering a Theology of the Call to Ordained Ministry for Women Today." *Theological Education* 39 (2003) 149–65.

Nouwen, Henri J. M. *In the Name of Jesus: Reflections on Christian Leadership*. New York: Crossroad, 1989.

Palmer, Parker. *Leading from Within: Reflections on Spirituality and Leadership*. Pamphlet. Indianapolis Office for Campus Ministry with support from the Lily Endowment, 1990.

Roxburgh, Alan J., and Fred Romanuk. *The Missional Leader: Equipping Your Church to Reach a Changing World*. San Francisco: Jossey Bass, 2006.

Schmidt, Jean Miller. *Grace Sufficient: A History of Women in American Methodism, 1760–1939*. Nashville: Abingdon, 1999.

# Pastoral Response

## Penny Rather

### Growing Pains

AT GATHERING AFTER GATHERING of ministers, I have heard colleagues declare, in all apparent sincerity, something like "Membership numbers are not the most important measure of a congregation's success." And, almost invariably, a little while later someone—sometimes the very same person—can be heard claiming quite proudly, "We had fourteen new members join last week!" Or, "Our congregation has grown by 25 percent in the past year!" Melanie Rosa's essay names and illustrates the tension between the need to "redefine what success in ministry looks like," and the "seductive temptations for women [ministers] eager to prove themselves." Since growth is often identified as a goal for congregations and denominations alike, it is worthwhile to consider what kinds of growth we are seeking and what kinds we are measuring and reporting.

In my understanding and experience of ministry, many kinds of growth are sought—growth in numbers, in spiritual maturity, in spiritual depth, and in capacity to effect the transformation of the world in which we live, to name a few. These spheres of growth are not unrelated, and I believe that greater spiritual maturity and depth ultimately lead to growth in numbers and influence in the world. But growth in numbers is so much easier to measure than other kinds of growth, and it reflects our culture's preference for traditionally masculine ways of assessing success, so this is what we most often report and pay attention to. Furthermore, the relationships among kinds of growth are multidirectional, and the growing number of women in ministry has increased awareness of and attention to the less measurable types of growth. The pains we endure in growing one aspect of ministry reap rewards in other areas as well.

As Rosa points out, "we must be careful about stereotyping female leadership," so an explanation of my use of language is in order here. Male and female, or man and woman, refer to biological classifications. For the most part humans are easily identified as male or female, though an understanding of transgender individuals is changing even this. Feminine and masculine, on the other hand, pertain to gender identification of qualities. Labeling of a characteristic as masculine or feminine is socially ascribed, and while there is a positive correlation between females (males) and feminine (masculine) qualities, typically both men and women exhibit feminine and masculine attributes. So the feminine qualities that Rosa claims are "desperately needed in a time when . . . the church is desperately trying to engage new generations" are brought to ministry by women and men who are in touch with their feminine traits. Moreover, appreciation for these qualities will mitigate the negative experiences of female ministers in a historically masculine system and will liberate *all* ministers to more fully appreciate and utilize their feminine strengths.

Rosa writes about the experience of women seminarians and ministers in mainline Christian churches, but her observations are valid in other faith communities as well. As a Buddhist practitioner and a Unitarian Universalist parish minister, I have observed a pattern similar to the one she reports in the United Methodist Church in both of these religious traditions. Unitarian Universalists are proud to claim as our own the first woman to graduate from theological school and be ordained with the full authority of a denomination (Universalist Olympia Brown, ordained in 1863). Women account for more than half of Unitarian Universalist clergy, and the trend is growing, with nearly three quarters of our seminarians being female. Yet, just as in the United Methodist Church, women serve fewer large churches, have fewer upper level leadership positions in our Association of Congregations, and typically earn less than their male counterparts. And while two of the characteristics of American Buddhism are the inclusion of women as equals in the community of practice and the adoption of traditionally feminine values,[1] women still lag behind men

---

1. Kornfield, "American Buddhism," xxiii.

in senior teaching and leadership positions. Even as I report the status of women leaders in Unitarian Universalism and American Buddhism, I recognize in myself a pull towards defining success with regard to the traditionally masculine metrics of numbers, size of churches served, and earnings. This inclination illustrates the "myth of competence" of which Rosa writes.

Rosa's exploration of a model of authentic leadership provides us with another, albeit less measurable, way to look at pastoral leadership. The characteristics she enumerates both affirm my understanding of leadership as informed by Unitarian Universalism and Buddhism and inspire me to remind myself and others to pay attention to these more traditionally feminine measures of success in ministry. In particular, the inner life of leaders and an experimental mindset reflect Buddhist practices and teachings around which my spiritual life and my ministry are woven.

The spiritual practice of meditation is central to my inner life and critical to my ministerial leadership. Daily mindfulness meditation, routine "specialty" meditations—such as a meditation on my own death—and regular (if all too infrequent) weeklong meditation retreats give me the opportunity and skills "to go deep within [myself] in order to lead with authenticity and power." All five of the "seductive shadows" of which Parker Palmer writes come up with regularity in meditation, and Buddhist teachings and practices help me deal effectively with them. For instance, the eight worldly *dharmas* (phenomena) "are four pairs of opposites—four things that we like and become attached to and four things that we don't like and try to avoid. The basic message is that when we are caught up in the eight worldly dharmas, we suffer."[2] Applying meditation on the pair of *dharmas* labeled "praise and criticism" to my preaching—recognizing that one sermon can, and often does, generate both of these responses—has been especially helpful in dealing with insecurity and fear of failure and has helped me let go of any "need to perform, impress, and produce results." And meditation on my own death reminds me that all phenomena are impermanent, constantly dying and being reborn moment to moment. This insight, understood experientially through meditation and not just learned intellectually, helps me appreciate the creative necessity of letting programs, traditions, or assumptions in my church die so that new and more effective ones may be born.

2. Chödrön, *When Things Fall Apart*, 59.

The experimental mindset of authentic leadership is reminiscent of the feminine principle in Tibetan Buddhism, which is insight into emptiness.[3] The Buddhist concept of emptiness tells us that all phenomena—including human and other beings, other material phenomena, thoughts, and feelings—ultimately lack any permanent, unchanging, independent essence. In other words, nothing lasts forever, everything changes, and all things and ideas are interdependent with other things and ideas. Leaders who have some insight into emptiness are willing to "upset and disrupt people, to constantly challenge equilibrium" and to "adapt quickly, improvise, and trust chaos" because they appreciate the creative potential of emptiness reflected in these approaches. Buddhism teaches that an effective spiritual path must include not only intellectual understanding of religious concepts, but also direct experience of spiritual truths, and it is through the spiritual practice of meditation that a practitioner can gain some experience of emptiness that informs authentic leadership as described by Rosa.

It is important to note that Buddhist teachings do not advocate the replacement of traditionally masculine approaches to leadership with feminine ones, but their integration. The masculine principle in Tibetan Buddhism is skillful means,[4] and these two principles can be viewed as the two wings of a bird, without both of which the bird cannot fly. But in our contemporary Western culture there is a need for an emphasis on the feminine principle and aspects of leadership traditionally associated with women to balance our historic overreliance on the masculine.

Finally, Rosa's introduction to two Methodist clergywomen reminds me of my interdependence with women of all traditions who paved the way for my ministry. These women remind me, too, of my responsibility to future clergy, both male and female, to promote a balanced approach to ministry that honors and makes use of *all* of our masculine and feminine gifts. When I wonder, as I sometimes do, just what I am doing in my ministry, or why I am doing it, these women's stories help me remember to ground my ministry in my faith and persevere through the growing pains—the aches and tenderness of personal and professional growth—for the benefit of those I serve.

---

3. Simmer-Brown, *Dakini's Warm Breath*, 51.

4. Ibid., 115.

# BIBLIOGRAPHY

Chödrön, Pema. *When Things Fall Apart: Heart Advice for Difficult Times.* Boston: Shambhala, 1997.

Kornfield, Jack. "American Buddhism." In *The Complete Guide to Buddhist America,* edited by Don Morreale, xxi–xxx. Boston: Shambhala, 1998.

Simmer-Brown, Judith. *Dakini's Warm Breath: The Feminine Principle in Tibetan Buddhism.* Boston: Shambhala, 2001.

# Chapter Seven

## Women's Experiences and Intercultural Spiritual Care

### Carrie Doehring

IN THIS CHAPTER I trace the theme of difference in the history of feminist pastoral care and theology in the past fifty years. During this time feminists began questioning whether women seeking pastoral care had unique needs hitherto unrecognized, and whether women pastors could hear and respond to these needs in ways different from their male counterparts. They paid attention to the particularities of women's experiences and began to hear the ways in which gender made a difference. They also began to hear how much the experiences of women of color—both pastors and care seekers—were shaped by racism. This process of listening closely to the unique experiences of women raised theological questions about God and suffering. These theological questions highlighted the limitations of abstract deductive theologies. Feminist pastoral theologians began developing experience-near inductive theologies that arose out of women's laments and protests against suffering. This ongoing exploration of difference has led to new ways of thinking theologically about and practicing care. In this chapter I will describe and illustrate one of these: the intercultural approach to spiritual care. I will highlight the ways in which it grapples with difference in today's global and religiously pluralistic context.

By tracing the history of how feminist pastoral theologians and caregivers have been jarred by and responded to the particularities of women's experience, this chapter honors the work of Jean Miller Schmidt, who explored the lived religion of ordinary Methodist women as narrated in their diaries, letters, and spiritual autobiographies, as well as in obituaries found in Methodist-related publications. By paying attention to what was unique about these women's experiences, Schmidt, like feminist pastoral theologians and caregivers, began to understand the history of Methodism differently.

## Listening for the Difference that Gender Makes: The Modern Approach

We begin our historical overview of feminist pastoral care with one of the hallmarks of the feminist movement in the United States in the 1960s: the consciousness raising of women as they put into words their experiences of being the so-called "second sex." The clarion call sounded in Simone de Beauvoir's 1949 manifesto by that name rallied women who were casting off traditional gender roles reaffirmed in the wake of the Second World War. The groundswell of change for women inaugurated by demands for equality and reproductive rights in the 1960s was like a tsunami that irrevocably changed the landscape of women's religious, professional, and familial roles.

The second wave of feminism in the United States extended the agenda for equality that propelled the first wave of the suffragette fight for equal voting rights at the beginning of the twentieth century. The women's rights movement beginning in the early 1960s focused on equal rights within the public realm where women had been denied equal educational opportunities and civil rights. Second-wave feminism also went beyond an agenda for equality by challenging and deconstructing patriarchy. It identified and valued the ways that women's and men's experiences were different, and then reformed or reconstructed patriarchal systems of meanings and practices by valuing women's ways of knowing and relating. This dual agenda of equality and reconstructing patriarchal systems energized feminist church leaders to dismantle overt and covert barriers to ministry and the ordination of women. An early expression of this agenda in feminist pastoral care was articulated by Peggy Way[1] and Emma Justes[2] who wrote in the 1960s and 70s about how sexism marginalizes women's ministry in the church.

When women assumed the functions of ordained leadership as liturgists, preachers, and pastoral caregivers, congregants often experienced the receptive, nurturing, and homemaking aspects of their ministry. In this process, patriarchal images of God and ministry were challenged and feminine dimensions of God and ministry were revealed in jarring or comforting ways. These feminist leaders chose to work within the historically patriarchal structures of their ecclesial traditions. They led the way in challenging and reforming the patriarchal aspects of their tradition without rejecting it. Feminist pastoral theologians articulated this agenda in the opening words of one of their first edited collections of essays: "Greater knowledge of women's experience, we believe, will enable all caregivers (both female and male) to provide better pastoral care by considering gender-specific presuppositions. This volume is a *new* pastoral care because it focuses on the gender needs of women."[3]

Listening to women's experience changed the way feminist caregivers theologically reflected on the stories of gender-related suffering they heard. Women pastors sensitized to the experience of gender violence began hearing themes of sexual violence in the stories women were telling them. They "heard into speech"[4] the previously unspeakable stories of rape, incest, and harassment. This phrase, used by feminist theologian Nell Morton, describes the process of women listening to women in an empathic compassionate way that helps them put into words their experiences of being "other" in male-dominated cultures and traditions. As women broke taboos that had silenced them in their families, communities of faith, and society and began speaking out about their experiences of sexual harassment, abuse, and assault, feminist pastoral theologians and caregivers grappled with profoundly disturbing theological questions about God, human nature, evil, and sin. Abstract, deductive systematic theologies that sought to justify how God could be all powerful, all know-

---

1. Way, "Women in the Church"; Way, "An Authority of Possibility for Women in the Church"; Way, "The Church and (Ordained) Women."

2. Justes, "The Church—For Men Only"; Justes, "Theological Reflections on the Role of Women."

3. Glaz and Moessner, *Women in Travail and Transition*, vi.

4. Morton, *The Journey Is Home*, 202.

ing, and all loving seemed designed to protect traditional doctrines rather than respond to the lament of survivors. Feminist pastoral theologians began constructing theologies from the underside of these experiences of violation. They drew upon inductive theologies that responded to laments of suffering and sought liberation and social transformation. Pastoral caregivers and seekers together searched for ways of experiencing a compassionate God who understood the desecration of sexual violation. For example, as Cooper-White observed, "some victims of rape and abuse have found hope in the crucifixion in the sense that, through his suffering, Jesus stands in solidarity with their suffering and there is no suffering that is unknown to God."[5] The search for meaning became a collaborative inductive process that engaged the jarring questions raised by the particularities of women's suffering.

## Listening for Contextual Differences:
## A Postmodern Approach

The consciousness raising among women in the United States that provided the groundswell for the second wave of feminism was soon followed by a growing articulation by African American women that white feminists could not speak for them. Neither feminist nor African American liberation theologies paid close enough attention to the compounded oppression of sexism and racism. Voices of Latina, Asian, African American, African, and lesbian women lamented the radical suffering particular to them. Once again, theological questions emerged. This time, theologies constructed out of the particular experiences of women of color raised questions about universal descriptions of women's experiences. The feminist theologies initially formulated in the second wave of feminism were based on the experiences of white, middle class women. Feminist and womanist theologians realized that any attempts to describe the essence of what it meant to be a woman were contextual. They described particular women whose experiences could not be generalized to all women.

This distinction between essentialist and contextual understandings of gender marked a shift from using modern to postmodern feminist approaches to understanding gender. Modern approaches to understanding women's experiences assumed that it was possible to reduce the vast

5. Cooper-White, *The Cry of Tamar*, 94.

diversity of narratives about what it meant to be a woman to a common core of feminine traits. The definition of womanhood generated by this structuralist approach was assumed to be universally and transhistorically true for all women. An example of essentialism can be found in numerous feminist theological reflections on women's development and life cycle stages that were popular in the 1980s.[6] These life cycle theories contrasted women's development and life cycle stages with those of men. Feminists pointed out that male psychologists used samples of boys and men in order describe human development. However, these feminists were guilty of describing the development of girls and women without paying attention the how other aspects of social identity like race, ethnicity, citizenship, sexual orientation and able-bodiedness influenced development and life cycle stages. Maxine Glaz and Jeanne Stephenson Moessner's first edited collection of essays[7] reflected second wave feminist perspectives that used modern psychological approaches to understanding women. They explored women's lifecycle transitions and crises arising from depression, reproductive health issues, sexual abuse, intimate partner violence, and work/family challenges. A subsequent publication edited five years later by Moessner[8] more explicitly reflects awareness of the ways that gender, race, class, and sexual and theological orientations shape women's experiences. These essays began to look more closely at contextual aspects of women's experiences.

Postmodern approaches to knowledge questioned the extent to which cultural traditions shape how aspects of humanity like gender are defined. They examined how the social location of those defining the essence of womanhood determined how gender was understood. Instead of assuming that that there was a common core experience of womanhood, postmodern feminists assumed not only that there were as many definitions of womanhood as there were cultures but also that, within each culture, there were as many definitions as there were social locations. For example, a Southern American male slave owner's definition of womanhood differed dramatically from how his wife or one of his female slaves defined womanhood, if these women were empowered to define for themselves their experience of being women. In other words, these

6. An example is Washbourne, *Becoming Woman.*

7. Glaz and Moessner, *Women in Travail and Transition.*

8. Moessner, *Through the Eyes of Women.*

definitions of what it meant to be a woman were socially constructed and shaped by their social location.

The shift from essentialist/modern to social constructionist/postmodern approaches to gender can be traced in the writings of many feminist pastoral theologians who began their work in the 1980s. This shift is explicitly elaborated in a theoretically oriented collection of essays on feminist and womanist pastoral theology edited by Bonnie Miller-McLemore and Brita Gill-Austern.[9] A more recent publication[10] moves back and forth between an essentialist/modern and social constructionist/postmodern orientation to gender. This resource explores approaches to pastoral care with socioeconomically vulnerable women, grieving African American women, Korean American women struggling with an inadequate sense of self, women with cancer, and American Indian women. Besides exploring the contextual ways that women suffer, authors describe multicultural approaches to pastoral care that pay attention to multiple structures of oppression, narrative strategies, and intergenerational dynamics.

## From a Clinical to an Intercultural Approach to Spiritual Care

This shift from essentialist to social constructionist understandings of gender was accompanied by a shift from clinical to contextual approaches to care. The clinical paradigm of pastoral care became popular among theologically liberal Protestant clergy and seminary professors in the 1950s. They relied upon the humanistic psychology and psychotherapeutic strategies of Carl Rogers.[11] Rogers' optimistic view of personality focused on self-actualization. His listening style of unconditional acceptance was a way of embodying God's compassion rather than God's judgment. For more liberal pastoral caregivers, the clinical paradigm was an appealing alternative to the classical/clerical paradigm of pastoral care. They wanted to replace traditional moral theologies of sin, suffering, and salvation with psychological theories and counseling that emphasized grace and human potential. The clinical paradigm reflected many modern American values: personal autonomy, individual freedom, and a belief in progress, along

9. Miller-McLemore and Gill-Austern, *Feminist and Womanist Pastoral Theology.*

10. Moessner and Snorton, *Women Out of Order.*

11. Rogers, *On Becoming a Person.*

with a nonmoralistic use of religion that focused on self-actualization and personal growth.[12] Feminist pastoral theologians initially used a clinical paradigm to focus on gender equality and self-actualization for women who were breaking out of traditional gender roles.

In the 1980s and '90s challenges to the clinical paradigm emerged from feminist and African American pastoral theologians and caregivers. While still embracing the liberal sensibilities that gave rise to the clinical paradigm, they questioned its often implicit white middle class values and subtle racist and patriarchal assumptions. By the turn of the twenty-first century, feminist challenges to the clinical paradigm were more explicitly using many of the following postmodern approaches to pastoral theology and care:

- the need for a relational and ecological understanding of God and created life

- a perspectival understanding of knowledge as socially constructed

- self-reflection about how one's social location and social privileges shape one's experience and knowledge

- a social, political, and theological analysis of the role of power and difference in human suffering and social injustice

- systemic strategies for pastoral and spiritual care in which individual, familial, and communal change is grounded in social justice.

These postmodern approaches were put into practice in an intercultural paradigm of spiritual care. An intercultural approach questions generalist theories and generic pastoral responses to women and pays attention to the unique aspects of each woman's story, religious experiences, and spiritual practices. An intercultural paradigm acknowledges the varieties of ways that care is practiced and understood throughout the world, and the need for building bridges between the cultures of the spiritual caregiver and care receiver.[13] In using an intercultural paradigm, feminist pastoral caregivers construct a contextual social analysis of whether and how being a woman of a certain social class, ethnicity, race, or age (etc.) yields social advantages and/or disadvantages. Examining the interplay of social identity and social privileges or disadvantages helps

12. Holifield, *A History of Pastoral Care*; Myers-Shirk, *Helping the Good Shepherd*.

13. Emmanuel Lartey was one of the first pastoral theologians to elaborate this paradigm.

pastoral caregivers think about how they might be judging those whose values and life experiences are different from their own. The following case study provides an example of intercultural spiritual care and will be used to make comparisons with a clinical approach to pastoral care.

## Case Study

Grace is fifty-year-old Caucasian associate pastor at Wesley United Methodist Church. In the coffee gathering after a Sunday evening innovative worship service she met Tiffany, a young African American woman, standing by herself. Tiffany had just enrolled as a college student at the beginning of the winter semester after relocating from a small town about 80 miles away. She delayed her studies because her father had died suddenly last August and, as the eldest in the family, she had wanted to be at home to help her mother. She had not had a chance to make friends with other students because she was living with a family and providing childcare as a way of supplementing her scholarship. Grace had the impression that Tiffany was shy and introverted, making Grace appreciate how difficult it must be for her to live off campus and enroll in the middle of an academic year. As they talked about her father's death, Tiffany described how important their African Methodist Episcopal (AME) church community had been. The pastor had helped her mother and the family experience a sense of ongoing spiritual connection with her father. Grace said that Tiffany would be very welcome to participate at Wesley while she was looking for an AME church home. She gave Tiffany a brochure listing the church's programs and highlighted the Open Door schedule: times during the week in which the pastors of the church welcomed people to drop by and talk over what was going on in their lives.

A few weeks later Tiffany stopped by during one of Grace's Open Door hours. Tiffany said hesitantly that she was worried about a course on writing that all entering students were required to take. She did not do very well on the first assignment. A few days ago she arranged to meet with Professor Nelson in order to go over the assignment. Professor Nelson had peppered her with questions: where she had gone to high school, what English literature courses she had done, what other universities she had applied to, and what led her to come to this university. Tiffany felt like she was questioning Tiffany's ability to be there. When Professor Nelson took a phone call during their conversation, Tiffany looked at the framed degrees on her wall, noting that one was from Harvard University. She wondered if she was, indeed, smart enough. Tiffany remarked that aside from this course, she had felt good about how her first semester was going and that she enjoyed the family with whom she was living.

Grace remarked at how well Tiffany had settled in and said she was curious about how Tiffany had coped with difficult situations in the past and whether she had ever had a similar experience with a teacher. Tiffany described how she had sought tutoring help in high school when a physics teacher was demanding and intimidating. Grace wondered whether Tiffany could find a similar kind of support. Tiffany thought her advisor, Rosa Manuela, might help her. She had told Tiffany that she had grown up in a small town in Arizona near the border and knew how hard to was to come to a large university.

Tiffany was quiet for a few minutes and then remarked that she really liked the sanctuary in the church. She had stopped by there before meeting Grace and found it very peaceful and beautiful, with the sunlight coming in through the stained glass windows, casting a glow over the communion table. She said she had prayed that she was doing the right thing before meeting with Grace, explaining that she did not want to be a complainer but knew she was worrying too much and that God was pushing her to reach out and not be alone. Her home church pastor often talked about God's spirit animating all things and beings; Tiffany wanted to feel this spirit in her life more deeply especially when she worried about this writing course. Grace echoed these wishes in the prayer Tiffany requested at the end of their conversation.

## A Reflection on the Case Study

This fictional illustration of spiritual care across age, class, and racial differences provides a framework for thinking about how feminist pastoral care has evolved over the past fifty years. In the 1960s and '70s the first feminist pastoral theologians would have focused on issues of sexism in this illustration, and highlighted how Grace's gentle responsive style of care reflected women's ways of knowing and relating. Using a clinical paradigm of care, Grace might have psychologically assessed Grace's struggles as an adjustment disorder that many women experience in the life cycle transition of leaving home and starting their college education. She might have planned a series of weekly counseling sessions that could look at underlying psychological causes for the kind of "low self-esteem" that so many women experience. It is easy to see in retrospect that even a feminist-oriented clinical approach focused on equal rights does not do justice to Tiffany's experience of racism, sexism and classism, nor to the challenges of pastoral care across race, class, and age differences.

In practicing an intercultural approach to spiritual care Grace uses contextual understandings of gender. She assumes that she and Tiffany will begin to explore what it means *for her* be an African American young woman with an AME upbringing, rather than relying on generalizations about what all young African American women experience. Grace cannot conclude, for example, that all African American women will be discriminated against at this university. Instead, the meanings that she or Tiffany co-construct are contextual and provisional (truth with a small *t* rather than Truth with a capital *T*). As British feminist pastoral theologian Elaine Graham put it, "principles of truth and value are not to be conceived as transcendent eternal realities, but as provisional—yet binding—strategies of normative action and community within which shared commitments might be negotiated and put to work."[14]

Grace could adopt a motherly role in trying to be an ally; her middle class, self-directed style might make her want to be in charge. In other words, the social privileges she has enjoyed might make Grace submerge Tiffany in Grace's white, middle class agenda. [15] This agenda, implicitly adopted in a clinical paradigm of care, often emphasizes how individuals can be "healed" and achieve self-actualization. Using an intercultural paradigm heightens Grace's awareness of her social advantages and the differences between her and Tiffany's social locations. This kind of social analysis will help Grace better empower Tiffany to interpret the possible subtle interplays of sexism, racism, and classism in her situation. An empowering relationship will also help Tiffany identify the values she holds dearest, which might include seeking social justice. Such values have become increasing important in the shift from a clinical to an intercultural paradigm of care, as Ramsay notes:

> Relational justice, normative for the communal contextual and intercultural paradigms, shifts the understanding of the self to a far more contextual, socially located identity in which the

14. Graham, *Transforming Practice*, 6.
15. Ramsay, "Where Race and Gender Collide."

political and ethical dynamics of asymmetries of power related to differences such as gender, race, sexual orientation, and class are prominent. From within the clinical pastoral paradigm pastoral counseling had long focused largely on liberating persons from spiritual and psychological bondage, but relational justice requires that care also includes attention to liberation from the actual bondage of oppression—the corollary of freedom from bondage is relational justice.[16]

As a postmodernist feminist pastoral caregiver, Grace could use the metaphor of a trifocal lens to describe the needs of someone like Tiffany. Grace might need an immediate sense of God's presence, using *precritical* ways of knowing. She also might need a better understanding of how others experience racism in the academy. She might turn to the internet to research these questions, using *modern* psychological, cultural and religious ways of knowing. Finally, over time she will need to develop intrinsic meanings and spiritual practices that are highly personal, in this way using *postmodern* ways of knowing.[17]

Grace might use the lens of premodern approaches to religious knowledge to assess whether Tiffany is yearning for an immediate sense of God's presence or a sense of the sacred. She might want to experience God in literal and concrete ways similar to how Christians experienced God in the premodern traditions. Tiffany's description of praying in the church sanctuary and experiencing a sense of peacefulness suggests that she is searching for an immediate sense of God's presence.

Grace can use a modern lens to assess whether Tiffany is ready or needs to understand her freshmen experience using a variety of modern theoretical perspectives from theological or psychological studies. For example, Grace could explore whether Tiffany wants to draw upon psychological research on prejudice. This research describes how an

16. Ramsay, "A Time of Ferment," 9.

17. Doehring, *The Practice of Pastoral Care*. A trifocal lens is useful in many cultural contexts where people shift among these different approaches to psychology and religious knowledge. As Lartey notes in his book *In Living Color* (40–41), "The pre-modern, modern and postmodern are present simultaneously in many places. The global reality is complex and diffuse. Whilst some discourse with a postmodern climate, others live in premodern conditions. Often these exist within the same locality. For many, the technological trappings of postmodernity sit alongside the pre-modern cultural assumptions, neo-colonial political forces, postcolonialist resistances struggles through art and music, and postmodernist frustration with globalized discourse. It is within this complexity that pastoral practitioners live."

African American in Tiffany's situation needs to be alert for possible discrimination, actively reject perceived stereotypes, and seek support.[18] Grace could also see if Tiffany is interested in psychological studies of how many African Americans find Afrocentric spirituality helpful in coping with racism.[19] Grace realizes she needs to review this research on how religion and spirituality can be helpful in reducing the effects of racism for Tiffany. If Tiffany is ready to turn to the Hebrew Bible or New Testament for help in meaning making, she can be encouraged to use a biblical critical approach in exploring how this source of authority can help her make sense of her life.

In the long-term process of helping Tiffany with meaning making, Grace can assess how Tiffany might start using a postmodern lens to articulate intrinsically meaningful religious experiences that emerge from Tiffany's particular cultural, communal, and family narratives.[20] Grace would like to become more familiar with how African American pastoral theologians like Carroll Watkins Ali[21] describe intercultural care across the racial, class, and age differences between Grace and Tiffany. This womanist pastoral resource will help Grace reflect upon the differences between her experiences/values and Tiffany's.

18. Branscombe et al., "Perceiving Pervasive Discrimination among African Americans."

19. Several psychological studies have used an African-centered epistemological framework for understanding and measuring how African Americans cope with racism. For example, Lewis-Coles and Constantine found that higher institutional racism-related stress was associated with greater use of cognitive/emotional debriefing, spiritual-centered, and collective coping in a study of almost three hundred African American women. Shorter-Gooden found that African American women coped with racism and sexism by using strategies that included self-affirming worldviews or belief systems, prayer, as well as connection to their heritage, to African and African American culture, and particularly to their ancestors. Similarly, Ellison, Musick, and Henderson found that daily religious practices like prayer and devotions as well as attendance at religious services buffers the effects of recent racist encounters on psychological distress. Drawing on the work of Pargament, Magyar, and Murray Swank on experiences of violation or desecration, Ellison, Musick, and Henderson suggest that racist encounters may represent a kind of desecration or violation of one's soul, and that religious practices and attendance may moderate the distress of soul-violating experiences of racism.

20. Williams and Wiggins, "Womanist Spirituality as a Response to the Racism-Sexism Bind."

21. Ali, *Survival & Liberation.*

## Conclusion

This case study illustrates the differences between feminist clinical and intercultural approaches to care. These two approaches have evolved in the past fifty years as feminist pastoral caregivers have paid attention to the particularities of women's experiences. Using a clinical approach, feminist pastoral caregivers focused on the differences between men's and women's experiences. They initially relied on emerging psychological research on gender differences and women's experiences of sexism, depression, low self-esteem, and sexual violence. They also constructed liberation theologies that responded to the kinds of suffering experienced by women.

This attention to the differences between men and women generated ways of understanding women's experiences that initially were liberating. By continuing to pay attention to differences, feminist pastoral theologians and caregivers soon realized the limitations of modern approaches to psychologically and theologically understanding women. At the same time, they acknowledged the white, middle-class orientation of the clinical paradigm of care, with its focus on healing or self-actualizing individuals through a series of one-on-one counseling sessions. They broadened their focus on gender differences to include all kinds of differences: racial, class, and sexual orientation, and many other aspects of social identity. This attention to difference found its fullest expression in postmodern ways of knowing and an intercultural approach to spiritual care. The creative and collaborative leadership of feminist pastoral theologians and caregivers began with the privileging of women's experiences, both as care givers and care receivers. Today it has evolved into an intercultural paradigm of pastoral care that does justice to the complex diversity of spirituality and suffering, as experienced by persons, families, communities, and social systems.

## BIBLIOGRAPHY

Ali, Carroll A. Watkins. *Survival & Liberation: Pastoral Theology in African American Context*. St. Louis: Chalice, 1999.

Beauvoir, Simone de. *The Second Sex*. Translated by Constance Borde and Sheila Malovany-Chevallier. New York: Knopf, 2010.

Branscombe, Nyla R. et al.. "Perceiving Pervasive Discrimination among African Americans: Implications for Group Identification and Well-Being." *Journal of Personality and Social Psychology* 77 (1999) 135–49.

Cooper-White, Pamela. *The Cry of Tamar: Violence against Women and the Church Response*. Minneapolis: Fortress, 1995.

Doehring, Carrie. *The Practice of Pastoral Care: A Postmodern Approach*. Louisville: Westminster John Knox, 2006.

Ellison, Christopher G. et al. "Balm in Gilead: Racism, Religious Involvement, and Psychological Distress among African American Adults." *Journal for the Scientific Study of Religion* 47 (2008) 291–309.

Glaz, Maxine, and Jeanne Stevenson Moessner "Preface." In *Women in Travail and Transition: A New Pastoral Care*, edited by Maxine Glaz and Jeanne Stevenson Moessner, vi–vii. Minneapolis: Fortress, 1991.

Graham, Elaine L. *Transforming Practice: Pastoral Theology in an Age of Uncertainty*. London: Mowbray, 1996.

Holifield, E. Brooks. *A History of Pastoral Care in America: From Salvation to Self-Realization*. Nashville: Abingdon, 1983.

Justes, Emma J. "The Church—For Men Only." *Spectrum* 47 (1971) 17–19.

———. "Theological Reflections on the Role of Women in Church and Society." *Journal of Pastoral Counseling* 36 (1978) 42–54.

Lartey, Emmanuel Y. *In Living Color: An Intercultural Approach to Pastoral Care and Counseling*. Rev. ed. London: Kingsley, 2003.

———. *Pastoral Theology in an Intercultural World*. Cleveland: Pilgrim, 2006.

Lewis-Coles, Ma'at E. Lyris, and Madonna G. Constantine. "Racism-Related Stress, Africultural Coping, and Religious Problem-Solving among African Americans." *Cultural Diversity and Ethnic Minority Psychology* 12 (2006) 433–43.

Miller-McLemore, Bonnie, and Brita Gill-Austern, editors. *Feminist and Womanist Pastoral Theology*. Nashville: Abingdon, 1999.

Moessner, Jeanne Stevenson, editor. *Through the Eyes of Women: Insights for Pastoral Care*. Minneapolis: Fortress, 1996.

Moessner, Jeanne Stevenson, and Teresa Snorton, editors. *Women Out of Order: Risking Change and Creating Care in a Multicultural World*. Minneapolis: Fortress, 2010.

Morton, Nelle. *The Journey Is Home*. Boston: Beacon, 1985.

Myers-Shirk, Susan E. *Helping the Good Shepherd: Pastoral Counselors in a Psychotherapeutic Culture, 1925–1975*. Baltimore: Johns Hopkins University Press, 2009.

Pargament, Kenneth I. et al. "The Sacred and the Search for Significance: Religion as a Unique Process." *Journal of Social Issues* 61 (2005) 665–87.

Ramsay, Nancy. "A Time of Ferment and Redefinition." In *Pastoral Care and Counseling: Redefining the Paradigms*, edited by Nancy Ramsay, 1–64. Nashville: Abingdon, 2004.

———. "Where Race and Gender Collide: Deconstructing Racial Privilege." In *Women Out of Order: Risking Change and Creating Care in a Multicultural World*, edited by Jeanne Stevenson Moessner and Teresa Snorton, 331–48. Minneapolis: Fortress, 2010.

Rogers, Carl. *On Becoming a Person: A Therapist's View of Psychotherapy*. Boston: Houghton Mifflin, 1961.

Schmidt, Jean Miller. *Grace Sufficient: A History of Women in American Methodism, 1760–1939*. Nashville: Abingdon, 1999.

Shorter-Gooden, Kumea. "Multiple Resistance Strategies: How African American Women Cope with Racism and Sexism." *Journal of Black Psychology* 30 (2004) 406–24.

Washbourne, Penelope. *Becoming Woman: The Quest for Wholeness in Female Experience*. San Francisco: Harper & Row, 1977.

Way, Peggy A. "An Authority of Possibility for Women in the Church." In *Women's Libera-tion and the Church: The New Demand for Freedom in the Life of the Christian Church*, edited by Sarah Bentley Doely, 77–94. New York: Association Press, 1970.

———. "The Church and (Ordained) Women." *Christian Ministry* 1 (1970) 19–22.

———. "Women in the Church." *Renewal* 4 (1964) 4–8.

Williams, Carmen Braun, and Marsha Wiggins. "Womanist Spirituality as a Response to the Racism-Sexism Bind in African American Women." *Counseling and Values* 54 (2010) 175–86.

# Pastoral Response

## Elizabeth Randall

### One Pastor's Journey

R EADING CARRIE DOEHRING'S "WOMEN'S Experiences and Intercultural Pastoral Care" is for me a humbling and hopeful window
through which to see the way I practice pastoral care. This article allows
me to examine my own experience of offering pastoral care for almost
thirty years now, and invites me to reflect on how I might become ever
more inclusive in my approach to those I will encounter in the years to
come. As I read, I remember some of the well-meaning errors of my
youth. I can also affirm those things I have learned, and which I hope are
now second nature. And then I look forward. The gift of this article for me
as a pastor is the challenge of going deeper. It calls me to reflect on how
reverently, respectfully, and carefully I am able to listen for the particularity of each person and the story that person entrusts to me.

Doehring reminds me of how I have come to understand the particularity of my own context, and how that context originally shaped my
approach to pastoral care. To say that I could be "Grace" in Doehring's
fictional case study begins to describe me. The second wave of feminism
influenced me profoundly as I was coming of age in the 1970s. Some of
my painful learning in college and seminary came through the angry or
patient efforts of women of color and lesbian women to point out how
my assumptions arose from my privilege. Beginning with what I learned
from them, and continuing as I lived and worked in the Third World, I
have become, I hope, ever more sensitive to difference and diversity. Still,

I understand that in some ways I will always be shaped by my modern concerns, and that it is only by conscious effort that I am able to embrace a postmodern approach to my vocation. That is where the insights of an article like Doehring's can help.

I see several immediate practical applications for me in the intercultural approach Doehring describes: in individual pastoral care, pastorally focused preaching, and pastoring groups through change. In each case, I think first about how I understand hope, future good, or salvation. While I have learned how to listen for and honor difference in another's experience, I often catch myself making assumptions about the other's desired future. This seems to me to be a theological and pastoral variation on "knowing what is best for you," and when I am mindful of it, I try to avoid it. But the assumption that I can know another's greatest good, because I believe I understand my own, is hard to shake.

I am surprised at where I encounter this most often. The cultural difference I am increasingly mindful of—now that I cannot avoid the knowledge that I entered middle age some time ago—is the gap between the generations. As a young and ardent feminist, and later as a young woman in ordained ministry, I was mindful of a gap between my experience and that of the very old. Still, we were all products of the modern era, whatever cultural and theological values we clung to. Now, in my work with young adults, I am aware of a cultural divide that to me seems profound, in some ways even more profound than the racial, socioeconomic, or political differences I have learned to be sensitive to in my pastoral encounters.

How can I listen carefully and respectfully to a young woman whose understanding of her potential and her future is so different from my own at her age? Can I recognize any hidden agenda I have for this person in this encounter? Is that agenda preventing me from listening, from seeing this person as herself, with her own needs, hopes and dreams? For instance, one of my own passions at her age was for gender inclusive language. I have come to understand—with a sense of loss—that my belief that words matter, and mean what they say, brands me as hopelessly modern in a postmodern world. How can I suspend my passion, and the belief that fuels it, while I listen for what she cares about? This is a place where Doehring's metaphor of the trifocal lens is compelling. If I am mindful of using that trifocal lens, I may hear a very simple, precritical longing, or hurt, or need, rather than remaining stuck in my critical perceptions. This young woman does not need someone to teach her "what is best for her."

She needs a pastor who can listen for who she is, what she has done, what has happened to her, and what she hopes.

In pastoral preaching, I know that I need to be sensitive to the examples I use. Who is left out of the stories I tell, as I attempt to show the divine engaged and active in our lives? Over the years I have learned, I hope, how to include more of the immense variety of human experience, rather than beginning simply with my own stories and the stories of people like me. That, however, is only the beginning. Preaching reaches beyond what we know and feel now, into the future we envision. Doehring reminds me that I also need to be mindful of how I describe the longed-for future.

My own longings, which are influenced by my particular context, are for meaning and freedom. When in my preaching I try to speak of salvation or redemption in nonreligious language, my first impulse is to speak of meaning and freedom. This is not necessarily the language that speaks to women, children, and men whose context is very different from my own. Safety, freedom from pain, access to food, shelter, education: these and many other things I have always taken for granted are concrete, tangible signs of salvation for others. If I speak of these things when I preach, I include more people. If I do not, I limit myself and my hearers.

Finally, in pastoring groups through change, I could help those among whom I work to become increasingly mindful. One way would be by helping them to examine how they want to grow. Often, when churches want to grow, they identify "becoming more diverse" as a strategy. Sometimes a group will make assumptions about what identified "others" will want, and make plans to meet perceived needs. Listening to others as individuals and seeing them through the "trifocal lens" often proves more effective, however. In Doehring's fictional case study, it is only when Grace listens without assumptions and sees through the trifocal lens that she is able to understand what Tiffany values about the church: the beauty of the sanctuary, the light, the quiet. Grace might help her congregation, if they wanted to know what programs would attract more "others" like Tiffany, to reflect instead on how they could welcome each individual and listen for her story. I, like Grace, might be able to help my congregation in the same way.

When I accepted the humbling privilege of offering pastoral care, I accepted the responsibility to examine myself and my work continually. Doehring, and her model of intercultural pastoral care, invites me to do this in new and familiar ways.

# PART THREE

## *Women and Scripture*

# Chapter Eight

## Zion as Refuge

### *A Metaphor with Implications for the Church in the Postmodern World*

### Amy Erickson

### Introduction

IN THEIR WORK ON metaphor, cognitive linguists George Lakoff, Mark Turner, and Mark Johnson have argued powerfully that metaphors are not merely poetic embellishments; they shape how we perceive, think, and behave.[1] Metaphors have conceptual power in that they serve to "create structure in our understanding of life."[2] These scholars and many others have concluded that we do not make metaphors—rather, metaphors make us.[3] Given the fundamental role of metaphor in shaping our perceptions about who we are, what we believe, and how we interact with the world around us, the mainline church in the postmodern world may

---

1. Lakoff and Johnson, *Metaphors*, 8.

2. Lakoff and Turner, *More Than Cool Reason*, 62.

3. Camp, "Metaphor in Feminist Biblical Interpretation," 34. See also Mac Cormac, *A Cognitive Theory*; Kittay, *Metaphor*.

find it valuable not only to examine the "metaphors we live by" but also to engage in conversation about the metaphors we *ought* to live by.[4]

I believe that the church could benefit from rediscovering and re-appropriating biblical metaphors as it steers a course into the future.[5] Metaphors from the modern period continue to inform the church's identity, not only in popular culture, but also the imaginations of pastors and congregations. Even churches that reject older models (i.e., "the church as a building" or "the church as a business") may still be left with somewhat of a vacuum when it comes to metaphors that define their mission and identity. Further, mainline churches in the U.S. are inevitably shaped, often subconsciously, by metaphors steeped deeply in American cultural values which do not always align with those of Christianity. Given what cognitive linguists say about how metaphors define and map reality for us, this is no small problem. Further, as linguist Suzette Hagen Elgin notes, the traditional way of dealing with metaphor is to sit and wait for one to appear *deus ex machina*.[6] Unless we begin to propose new metaphors for the church we will continue to be defined by old or inappropriate ones. Indeed Elgin boldly asserts that she believes metaphors to be "the only efficient way to bring about real change in human attitudes."[7]

I would like to suggest that the metaphor of Zion as a refuge—though not wholly unproblematic—could be a useful place for leaders, women leaders in particular, to begin thinking about how they might rename and re-imagine the role and function of the mainline church in the postmodern United States. Therefore in this article I will explore several of the motifs evident in the "Zion as refuge" metaphor in the Psalter.[8] My focus will be on the Zion Songs or Hymns (Psalms 46; 48; 76; 84; 87; 122; 132; 147).[9] While I will use theories of metaphor to analyze the components

---

4. Lakoff and Johnson, *Metaphors*.

5. The Pauline metaphor of the body of Christ is a good example of a revitalized biblical metaphor for the church.

6. Elgin, "Response," 209–17.

7. Ibid., 211.

8. The image of refuge plays a prominent role in the Psalter. Jerome Creach, in his study on the editing of the book of Psalms, maintains that refuge is a recurring idea or root metaphor in the book of Psalms. Similarly, Brown describes the refuge metaphor as one of the broadest metaphorical schemas or contexts in the Psalter, in which a number of images have their roots (Creach, *Yahweh as Refuge*, 18; Brown, *Seeing the Psalms*, 19).

9. Hermann Gunkel was the first to isolate a set of psalms as modified "hymns," which he deemed "Songs of Zion" (Pss 46, 48, 76, 84, 87, 122). These hymns are similar

of the metaphor, feminist and postcolonial hermeneutics also inform the study.[10] I maintain that the metaphor of Zion as refuge is a rich and multifaceted one that has the potential to inject a dose of imagination into the mainline church's self-understanding and to be life-giving to women in leadership positions in the church.

That said, using the Hebrew Bible as a touchstone when offering a constructive vision of community for contemporary women can be daunting because it entails navigating the patriarchal and imperial landmines in the Hebrew Bible. We have learned from centuries of biblical interpretation that biblical texts and the metaphors contained therein can be used (and have been used) to promote and justify violence and oppression. Feminist, Womanist, and postcolonial interpreters, in particular, are acutely aware of the ways the Bible has been used as a weapon to beat women, indigenous people, Jews, Muslims, and countless other groups of people. Therefore it is essential for biblical interpreters doing constructive work to expose potentially colonial, imperial, and/or misogynist appropriations of a biblical text or metaphor. Acknowledging problematic interpretations (past and potential) can help Euro-American churches reflect on the many ways it has contributed to violence and help non-Euro-American churches assess theological constructions that have contributed to their experiences of oppression.

At the same time, acts of textual deconstruction are not sufficient. As Silvia Schroer argues, "the call for more constructiveness is an urgent appeal to feminist exegetes to transform creatively their important critical analysis so as not to remain merely de-constructive but to introduce orientation and constructiveness to their work."[11] Further the mainline church in the postmodern world is in desperate need of renewal. And metaphors in the Hebrew Bible may be able to help churches both root

---

in form to hymns, but Gunkel distinguished them based on their distinct subject matter and their shared *Sitz im Leben*, which he presumed to be a cultic celebration of the glory of Jerusalem. Also Ollenburger points out, these Psalms do not represent a distinct formal category (*Gattung*); nor do they represent a "general doctrine of Zion's inviolability" (Ollenburger, *Zion, the City*, 16). They also do not function as a systematic exposition of the meaning of Zion or the tradition of its unique status.

10. Claudia Camp argues that a metaphor theory that is grounded in cognitive linguistics "can provide further theoretical grounding for the critical use of experience and embodiment in feminist analysis by demonstrating their contribution to the making of meaning in general" (Camp, "Metaphor," 4–5).

11. Schroer, "'We Will Know Each Other,'" 13.

themselves in tradition and re-imagine themselves with passion and openness in the context of a new and diverse world.

In order to try to balance the need for both deconstruction and reconstruction, in this essay, I will explore the problematic aspects of this metaphor as well as its potentially constructive applications.[12] After outlining the basic contours of the Zion as refuge metaphor, I will focus on four particular motifs of the metaphor that I think have the potential to be life-giving for communities who might adopt it as a means to reflect on their own identities and roles in the world. Through this exploration of Zion as haven in the midst of chaos, Zion as community of the righteous, Zion as a place and symbol of peace, and Zion as mother, we can begin to imagine ways in which this ancient metaphor might bring new life into Christian communities today.

## The "Zion as Refuge" Metaphor: Basic Contours

In the Hebrew Bible, the symbol of Zion signifies God's choice of a dwelling in Jerusalem. The ideology of Jerusalem, as well as the temple and the royalty associated with the city, centered around the belief that Zion was God's chosen abode, that YHWH's presence permeated that location and that from there God poured out blessing upon God's people.[13] In Psalm 132, the psalmist's words explain the correlation between YHWH's choice for Zion and the implications of that choice for its residents: "For YHWH has chosen Zion; God has desired it to be a dwelling for God's self. 'This is my resting place forever, here I will dwell for I have desired it. I will bless greatly her provisions. I will satisfy her poor with bread' (Ps 132:13–15)."[14]

The idea that Zion is God's abode depends on strong mythological links between the city of Zion and the concept of holy mountain on which God sets his throne.[15] In the Psalter, Zion is associated, directly and

12. In his insightful work on violence and the Bible, John J. Collins concludes that although the Bible has been used to justify violence throughout history, the content of the Bible itself—or any religious text—is not the problem per se. Rather it is certitude regarding the Bible's interpretation that contributes to violence in the world. He says, "perhaps the most constructive thing a biblical critic can do toward lessening the contribution of the Bible to violence in the world is to show that such certitude is an illusion" (Collins, *Does the Bible*, 33). See also Collins, "The Zeal of Phineas," 11–33.

13. Clements, *God and Temple*, 71.

14. All translations are the author's unless otherwise noted.

15. This mythological conceptualization of Zion is rooted in Canaanite Mount Zaphon

indirectly, with the mighty, immovable mountain of God, rooted in the depths of the earth, standing stalwart against the forces of chaos that surround it. In Israelite thought, Zion lies at the center of the world, its base reaching into the depths of the underworld and its peak stretching into the heavens. Like other temples in the ancient world, for Israel and Judah, Jerusalem was the *axis mundi*, the connecting point between heaven and earth.[16] From this solid position in the cosmos, the psalmist proclaims:

> God is for us a refuge and a strength,
> God is truly found to be a help in distress.
> Therefore we do not fear when the earth changes,
> When the mountains shake in the heart of the sea,
> Its waters roar and foam,
> And the mountains quake at its pride.
> God is in her [Zion's] midst, she will not totter
> God helps her at the break of dawn. (Ps 46:1–3, 5)

Given its rootedness in the depths of the earth and the security offered by God's presence, Zion is often depicted as a fortress. In Psalm 48, God and the fortress/city of Zion are so closely linked that at the conclusion of the psalm (vv. 13–15), it becomes apparent that YHWH himself has taken on the attributes of the city[17] ("Walk about Zion . . . For *this* is God, our god, forever and always"). As Brown notes, "the psalmist is not so crass as to make God into a building. Rather, the psalmist claims God's saving presence as palpably firm, permanently indwelling, and all-encompassing."[18] It is not the physical structure of Zion that affords its inhabitants this security. It is YHWH's presence that ensures the safety of the city. This perception of God's power and protection allows the worshipper to interpret ordinary signs of physical protection as infallibly secure. Not unlike the bread and wine of the Eucharist, the ordinary structures of an ancient Mesopotamian city could function as symbols of God's nearness. Just as Jesus the Christ becomes present to those who receive the Eucharist in the bread and the wine, for those who worship in Zion, YHWH becomes present through the city itself.

---

(Ps 48:3–4), the location of the storm and warrior god Baal's temple, which he constructs after he defeats Yamm ("Sea"), the personification of chaos. For more background, see Clifford, *The Cosmic Mountain*; Roberts, "The Davidic Origin," 313–30.

16. Eliade, *The Myth*.

17. Ollenburger, *Zion, the City*, 74.

18. Brown, *Seeing the Psalms*, 23.

The theological claim of divine presence in Zion is a powerful one. Indeed the claim that "God is in our midst" can lead to the dangerous assumption that we (alone) have God on our side. Such a triumphalist attitude has vexed the church throughout its history, particularly in wake of Constantine. And yet, ultimately the Zion tradition's emphasis on creation and on Zion's position vis-à-vis that creation functions to relativize Israel's individual, "historical" experiences of God's salvation. The creation theology that permeates the Zion tradition implies that God's care, providence, and future vision do not pertain strictly and narrowly to Israel alone. God determines the futures of the nations apart from any direct relationship with or connection to Israel (cf. Deut 32:8–9 and Psalm 82).[19] Thus the cosmic web of associations that underlie the Zion metaphor ultimately undermines any imposition of universal standards on other nations. Sitting at the fulcrum of heaven and earth, Zion is like a portal linking heaven and *all* creation, functioning as both a microcosm and as a pointer to the holiness of all creation.[20]

The metaphor of Zion as God's dwelling place is rich in the sense that God is not exclusively available to "us" in a particular geographical location but palpably present in creation. And yet, the community in Zion experiences that presence specifically and locally in its particular context. This kind of localized expression of divine presence is particularly relevant to the church in the postmodern world, in which generalizations and metanarratives (or "grand stories") are no longer as compelling as they were in the era of the enlightenment.[21] In the following sections, I will explore four elements of the Zion metaphor and suggest ways that the church might consider ways to appropriate the metaphor into its understanding of its mission, role, and function in the world.

---

19. Roberts, "The Enthronement," 675–86.

20. To counter a history of violent and oppressive biblical interpretation, Canaan Banana calls for interpreters to start from the presupposition that holiness pervades all of God's creation and that God is present in all creation. Based on this assertion that all creation is holy, in this article, Banana ultimately argues for expanding the canon to include texts from numerous traditions and cultures (Banana, "The Case," 21).

21. Lyotard, *The Postmodern Condition*.

## Four Elements of the Metaphor of Zion

### Zion as a Haven in the Midst of Chaos

As we have seen, in some of the Zion Songs, notably Psalm 48, one aspect of the refuge metaphor is that of the fortress. In Psalm 48, the psalmist enjoins the gathered community to walk about Zion, count its towers, consider its ramparts, and go through its citadels (vv. 12–13a). Zion is extolled as a place that protects its inhabitants by inspiring fear in those who would seek to attack it (vv. 4–7).

Appropriated by the church, this image of Zion the fortress could lead the church to envision itself as a space set apart from the world, safely walled off from the chaos around it. If the elect are safe within the walls of God's presence (particularly if they view themselves as chosen to reside in "Zion" on account of their righteousness), the rest of the world need not concern them. Further, because this space is holy, the church, imagined this way, also may become concerned with keeping what it judges to be the less godly aspects of the world out. Many churches are vexed by the question of who is welcome inside the "fortress" and who is not.

It strikes me as significant for the church that Zion is depicted as a haven set apart from, yet *in the midst* of, fear and chaos. It is a place that—because of the felt presence of God—is able to transform chaos into energy and life. The structure of Ps 46:2–8 points to this image of Zion as a protected and protecting island surrounded by chaotic and threatening seas. Ps 46:3–4 and 7–8 depict the forces of chaos that threaten life and order. The central verses (vv. 5–6), however, portray the waters as divinely transformed from threat to life-giving force.[22] Significantly, it is God, not the human community, who transforms the threat. Further, the inhabitants of Zion are not charged to be gatekeepers, deciding which elements are allowed in and which are not.

The church, guided by this image of Zion, might imagine itself as a place that does not run from the chaos but enables its transformation—not on its own but by welcoming God into its midst, by recognizing God's desire to heal and gather, and in turn creating a haven for all those who fear, suffer and are oppressed: "YHWH builds Jerusalem; the outcasts of Israel, God gathers. God heals the ones with broken hearts and bandages their wounds" (Ps 147:2–3). The church might imagine itself as a community

---

22. Tsumura, "The Literary Structure," 29–55.

charged to create a space symbolizing that refuge is available to all and that it is God's intention to expand and extend refuge to all creation.

Finally, although Zion is associated with Jerusalem, Zion does not refer solely to the temple space (or by analogy, to the church building), for Zion is variously located in the Hebrew Bible. It is identified with the holy mount (Ps 2:6), the sanctuary (Ps 20:3), the temple precinct (Pss 48:13; 46:5), God's dwelling place (Ps 48:2), and the city in its entirety (Pss 48:13; 46:5). While Zion is clearly in view in Psalm 46, the fact that the word "Zion" is not used in Psalm 46 at all seems to communicate that the city of God is not limited to Jerusalem or even to the idea of Zion: "God is in the midst of her/She will never be moved" (Ps 46:5). The community is defined not by its walls or its boundaries but by the presence of God discernible therein. Reminiscent of the "tabernacling" tradition, even in Zion, God's presence cannot be pinned down; nor is the mountain sanctuary set apart from the city and the people who live in it.[23]

## *Zion as a Community of the Righteous*

Another feature of the Zion metaphor is that God's holy presence in Zion entails particular demands on those who dwell in the midst of the divine presence (Pss 15; 24:3–6; see also Isa 33:13–16). Righteousness and justice are not merely cultivated in Zion; at the foot of God's holy throne, they are demanded.

The history of the Christian church's interpretation of Zion texts can provide an important cautionary for anyone who might wish to appropriate these metaphors. Beginning with the church fathers, promises to and praises of Zion were interpreted as applying to Christians—in place of Jews.[24] Because pre-Enlightenment Christians tended to believe that the Jews were rejected as the chosen people because of their refusal to accept

23. Brueggemann contrasts the traditions associated with David and with Moses, and argues that the two take fundamentally different theological and sociological trajectories. These two traditions represent, on the one hand, traditional tribal leadership (Moses), and on the other, the bureaucratic leadership of the monarchy (David). Brueggemann argues that the older Mosaic "tradition of 'tent' asserts a claim of mobility and freedom for God. The 'house' tradition is surely royal in its orientation and stresses the abiding presence of Yahweh to Israel" (Brueggemann, "Trajectories," 23). The reference to a tabernacling tradition is intended to evoke Brueggemann's tent tradition.

24. Rossing says, "ultimately, their [Jews and Christians'] dispute over the meaning of Zion as the city of God reflects rival claims to be the true Israel, or people of God, the chosen forebears of the future" (Rossing, "Zion," 450–51).

Jesus Christ as the messiah, many Christians felt justified in stripping away Jewish identification with Zion and applying it to themselves as "replacement people" who are more disciplined and more spiritual and simply superior to Jews.[25] Accordingly, the metaphor of the church as Zion was, for centuries, heavily tinted with supersessionism and Christocentrism. Being in Zion meant being chosen, not out of God's freedom, as election is depicted in the Hebrew Bible, but as a result of and reward for human merit and right belief. Therefore the church as Zion implied a belief in the ethical and spiritual superiority of a particular group of people.

And yet, while the metaphor itself may be prone to such abuse, the metaphors of Zion in the Hebrew Bible emphasize, not human accomplishment and divine reward, but human vulnerability and divine grace and sovereignty. Those who "live" in Zion are expected to live their lives as a response to God's gift of refuge. The vision of perfection in Zion is fueled by faith in God who will bring peace to all the world. And yet, in Zion, there are ethical demands made of the human community. These demands are not clearly and specifically enumerated; rather, the contours of an ethical response to living gratefully in YHWH's presence are sketched poetically and somewhat abstractly.

## Attitude of Trust

The fundamental ethical demand on inhabitants of Zion is that they cultivate an attitude of radical trust in YHWH. "Those who trust in YHWH are like Mount Zion" (Ps 125:1–2). As William Brown notes, "'refuge' is made real, or embodied, through the community's trust in God, and reciprocally, through God's protective care."[26] The refuge provided in Zion elicits a response of wholehearted trust from the people who experience divine protection therein. Such a response is typical of "the poor," who are accustomed to relying on YHWH for security, in part because, unlike the rich or the proud, they have no resources at their disposal to disavow them of the notion that God alone provides true refuge.[27] Ben Ollenburger argues that in Zion, the working distinction is not between the enemies—those who commit acts—and the righteous but between

25. Clark Williamson analyzes Tertullian's doctrine of the church, in which he refers to God "transferring his favor" from the Jews to the church (Williamson, *A Guest,* 235–45).

26. Brown, *Seeing the Psalms,* 25.

27. Ollenburger, *Zion, the City,* 70.

"the poor" who trust in YHWH alone and the arrogant who trust only in their own wealth, metaphorically or literally (see Pss 9:11; 10:6, 14; 40:5, 18; 46:6; 86:1–2). In texts that highlight the Zion tradition, the sin consistently highlighted is pride; pride being defined clearly as depending on one's resources rather than on YHWH.[28]

## Care for the Vulnerable

As the community in Zion experiences protection, it also extends it to others in need. Those in need are variously depicted as Israelites, outsiders, and even animal creatures. Psalm 84 emphasizes that all of God's creatures are protected in Zion.

> Even the birds find a home there,
> and the swallow builds a nest,
> where she can protect her young
> near your altars, O YHWH who rules over all,
> my king and my God. (Ps 84:3)

Psalm 147 emphasizes God's care and concern for the poor, the outcasts, and the wounded (vv. 2–3), as well as for the animals ("God gives to the animals their food, and to the young ravens when they cry," v. 9). Zion is like a luxury hotel turned animal rescue center/homeless shelter/orphanage/battered women's shelter.

In Zion, YHWH is the ruler who provides perfect refuge for those in trouble. However, there is also a human king in Jerusalem/Zion, who, in a sense, functions as YHWH's representative on earth. The king's role as protector of the needy is emphasized in royal theology as well as in texts describing kingship throughout the ancient Near East.[29] It was also the human king's duty to ensure that justice was properly meted out in God's city. The king's performance was ultimately assessed according to the model provided by the divine king.

In the Zion songs, the imagery suggests that divine representation is democratized to a degree. The Zion songs, while they may presume the presence of a king, do not emphasize the role of the human king.

---

28. Ibid.

29. Patrick Miller observes that in the final shape of the Psalter, the prayer for the weak, needy and sick first appears in Pss 9–10, "and that happens with such vigor that it places the protection and support of the poor and the needy as the fundamental content of the sovereignty of God" (Miller, "The Ruler in Zion," 176).

Ethical demands made on the king in the royal psalms are extended to the community as a whole in the Zion Songs. As Roberts notes, as with the king, the "idealization of Jerusalem in the Zion theology provided a basis on which the real Jerusalem of any particular period could be measured and criticized as not living up to the ideal." [30] Thus the standards of justice and righteousness were higher and more stringent in Zion in order to give proper honor and praise to the holy God who was believed to reside there. As Jon Levenson eloquently puts it, ". . . a text like Psalm 24 indicates that, properly conceived, the Temple is a place of electrifying holiness that cannot tolerate injustice." [31]

And yet, because there are stringent ethical expectations of the community, it does not follow that those who dwell in Zion have achieved, or can by their own actions achieve, perfection. [32]

## Participation in the Holy

Although visions of utopia and human perfection abound in the Zion Songs, of course, no real flesh and blood human worshipper is a model of perfect righteousness, nor is she expected to be. At the foot of Mount Zion, one pledges allegiance to the ideal. One suspends visions of reality for the visions of God's new creation. Entering Zion, climbing the hill, was a means to enter an out of the ordinary existence, characterized by proximity to God. Here at this metaphorical fulcrum of heaven and earth one could experience a form of paradise, a sense that s/he is in sync simultaneously with God and creation. [33] By trusting in God and by living out that trust, ethically, one can "partake of the creative and transforming energy that radiates from the Temple atop Mount Zion." [34]

30. Roberts, "The Enthronement," 685.

31. Levenson, *Sinai and Zion*, 170.

32. The history of interpretation reveals that the Zion tradition has been associated with confidence in human progress. American historian J. Larry Hood describes John Milton as one who "blended the vitality and new hope of the Renaissance with a Protestant emphasis on [Old Testament] prophecy and envisioned an apocalyptic progressivism in which people were marching to an end time of righteousness" (Hood, *Visions of Zion*, 2). Rooted in this type of belief in progress evident in seventeenth-century England, American Protestants around 1900, in undertaking great reforms, also viewed themselves as God's people walking the path God had laid out for them.

33. Levenson, *Sinai and Zion*, 175.

34. Ibid.,174.

And when one imaginatively enters Zion, one experiences not only protection but also bounty and beauty. In Ps 48:9, the one who walks about Zion has a sensual and visual experience of divine protection. In Ps 36:8–10, Zion is presented as a place of refuge from the harsh realities of daily life.[35] This haven is imagined as a place where God shares food and drink with those who have gathered there. As Jon Levenson says, "Zion represents the possibility of meaning, out of history, through an opening into the realm of the ideal. Mount Zion, the Temple on it, and the city around it are a symbol of transcendence, a symbol in Paul Tillich's sense of the word, something 'which participates in that to which it points.'"[36] In Zion, we are invited to "taste and see that YHWH is good" (Ps 34:8). The Zion Songs portray and offer a fundamentally sensual experience of God's love and care. The experience of proximity to God, of living into the call to be Zion for the world, is elating and enlivening. Worshippers long for Zion because it is a place of joy (Ps 82:3) and the "perfection of beauty" (Ps 50:2). People long to be in Zion because there they experience the beauty and wonder that emanates from God's presence.

The implications for church are important. One of the goals of worship could be to provide the sensual experience of being transported, of nearness to God. Having participated with and experienced the holy, one can return to the world of the mundane with a new energy. Fed by the feast in Zion, the worshipper is filled and ready to feed the hungry.

In its history, the Protestant church has tended to underestimate the significance of worship as a ritual experience designed to transport one into the glorious, bountiful presence of God. Providing experiences filled with beauty and bounty not only energizes worshippers, it can be lifesaving. Elaine Scarry is a philosopher who has written on the relationship between beauty and justice. She says, "Beauty quickens. It adrenalizes. It makes the heart beat faster. It makes life more vivid, animating, living, worth living."[37] Scarry goes on to argue that the perception of beauty leads to a "radical decentering." She says that "all the space formerly in the service of protecting, guarding, advancing the self (or its 'prestige') is now free to be in the service of something else."[38] Shifting the focus away from

---

35. Ibid., 132, 174.

36. Ibid., 142.

37. Scarry, *On Beauty*, 25

38. Ibid., 113.

the self leads to the site of stewardship, "in which one acts to protect or perpetuate a fragment of beauty already in the world or instead to supplement it by bringing into being a new object."[39]

## Zion as a Place and Symbol of Peace

Jerusalem is the "city of peace." God's presence in Zion affects a beatific life, characterized by joy, peace, and security for those dwelling in Jerusalem.[40] In Psalm 122, prayers for peace in Jerusalem are spoken. And in other psalms, God destroys all weapons and implements of war (Pss 46:8–9; 76:3; 76:5–6[6–7]); "he makes wars cease to the ends of the earth" (Ps 46:9). Peace is God's desire for Jerusalem both as a city and as a microcosm of all creation.

While visions of peace and wholeness in Jerusalem are appealing, at times it is evident that an imperial ideology underlies these visions. As Jim Roberts points out, the conceptual world behind texts such as these is that of an imperial state centralized in the city of Jerusalem.[41] Such an imperial vision of peace may entail that all those on the outside are destroyed because they are heathen—or they must be converted. [42]

Historically, Israel was itself dominated, colonized, exploited and, for most of its history, largely incapable of destroying, never mind converting, the nations. However, Muse Dube argues that texts from the Hebrew Bible, as well as the New Testament, have adopted the imperialist views of its oppressors, in particular by advocating "the structural imposition of a few standards on a universal scale."[43] These aspects of the Zion metaphor that appear to promote the conversion of non-Judeo-Christians have the potential to reinforce problematic imperial agendas associated with colonialism's long and troubled history.[44]

And yet, while Dube and Roberts make important points, precisely how the Zion tradition imagines the role of the nations and how they

39. Ibid., 114.

40. Levenson, *Sinai and Zion*, 148–51.

41. Roberts, "The End of War," 119–28.

42. Dube, "'Go Make Disciples,'" 224–54.

43. Ibid., 233. See also Kwok, *Discovering the Bible*, 8–14.

44. Dube, "'Go Make Disciples,'" 224. One should note, however, that the metaphor does not conceive of Israel as disavowing the borders of the nations in order to extract desirable resources and to exploit an alien people. Instead the nations come to Zion and reap the benefits of the *shalom* within the city of God.

are incorporated (or not) into Zion is highly ambiguous. For example, in Psalm 87, a psalm that employs the image of Zion as mother, it is particularly difficult to describe how Israel imagines its future ideal relationship with the nations. Some scholars see Psalm 87 as a text that represents a universal expansive view of Yahwism.[45] Others maintain the opposite view, arguing that Psalm 87 is determinedly nationalistic, solely concerned with encouraging Jewish identity in the Diaspora rather than promoting universalism.[46] Ultimately, Psalm 87—and the Zion Songs as a whole—is ambivalent, or at least ambiguous, about the relationship between Zion and the nations.

With a proper awareness of the potential imperializing applications of this metaphor, visions of *shalom* in Zion can play a role in the church's self-understanding. Roberts argues that in their historical context, these visions functioned to call the community to solidarity and to recommit themselves to the righteous requirements of YHWH. Visions of a glorious, abundant peace provide encouragement, even in an uncertain present, to create and maintain communities rooted in the Yahwistic demands of justice and righteousness.[47] In an uncertain and frightening present, the mainline church may be tempted to function from a place of fear and out of a desire for self-preservation. The vision of peace in Zion can provide the church with a vision of a community life, driven not by fear or anxiety but rooted in trust and commitment to the ideals associated with that vision of peace.

The vision of peace may also function to place in perspective the military and economic prowess of the powerful. Even when bowing to the demands of these powers seems to be the only way to survive, the community is urged to trust in God's grander vision of the future and to live

45. Sorg, *Ecumenic Psalm*. Similarly, Christl Maier maintains that Psalm 87 casts Zion as the spiritual mother of all peoples, and therefore breaks with the Zion tradition's nationalist roots (Maier, *Daughter Zion*, 209).

46. Stadelmann, "Psalm 87," 333–56.

47. J. J. M. Roberts points out that while many Christian ethicists maintain the centrality of the New Testament's pacifism, the New Testament writing emerged from a period in which the faith community had no control over its political (national or imperial) existence. Roberts concludes, "The early Christians were not responsible for governing the state, and even if they had desired, they were unable to project political power to benefit anyone... One should think twice, therefore, before dismissing the witness of that part of the canon that actually addresses believers who, like us . . . have the power and responsibility to govern according to God's will" (Roberts, "The End of War," 128).

in accordance with that vision. When Israel (and we) places its trust in military strength, wealth, and influence, the community loses sight of the vision God has for it and for the world. Living out of trust in God's promises and living into God's vision of peace the world over allows the church to stand as a steady force for hope in a chaotic world precariously perched atop complex and shaky alliances, shifting ideals and fleeting visions.

The image of the nations and kingdoms tottering and toppling might also have a valuable function if we understand it in an allegorical sense. In a postmodern world in which the very structures that have defined and upheld the church for centuries seem to be collapsing around us, the faithful community need not cling to these crumbling towers. In Psalm 46, the community in Zion finds its center in God's presence. The people with God witness the collapse of the world as they know it, and they stand as witnesses to the violence and destruction of the historical and mythic forces of chaos. They witness all this, feeling the ground beneath their feet tremble and shake, knowing that in the end, this god of destruction is working to spread the idea of Zion outward to encompass the nations and cover the world with this tent of peace first pitched on Zion.[48] Obviously this is not a new world achieved without cost. But to those who would attempt to hasten such an apocalypse, the psalm is defiant: "Stop your striving and recognize that I am God" (Ps 46:10). God will cause the seed of peace planted on Zion to grow throughout the earth, so that all creation might be called Zion.

The waters of chaos, evil kingdoms, and forces of change all beat on Zion's walls, but the command to the community is to rest, be still, and stop striving. God's vision of a future for God's creation is one of peace, abundance, and joy. In the meantime there is a Zion—a haven and a refuge, a place where one can simply be still and know that God is God. This image may be useful for the church in that Zion functions as a place where justice and peace are cultivated. Zion is also a place that nurtures, heals, renews and restores (Pss 36:8–10; 147:2–3, 8, 14).

---

48. Artur Weiser says that in the presence of God, the members of this cult community recognize their place in the formation and dissolution of creation. "Even though the world perishes and 'changes' (this is the literal translation) its shape, whilst the last days emerge with terrible labor pains . . . this total collapse of the finite cannot frighten the faithful" (Weiser, *The Psalms*, 368).

## Zion as Mother

In the context of the Zion Songs as group, Psalm 87 presents Zion with a different nuance.

> I will proclaim[49] Rahab and Babylon as ones who know me[50]
> Even Philistia and Tyre with Cush—(I will proclaim) "This one
>     was born there."[51]
> And of Zion it is said, "Each one was born in her."
> And Elyon makes her secure.
> YHWH writes in the book of the peoples
> "This one was born there." (vv. 4–6)

This key section of the psalm is enigmatic to say the least, and yet some scholars claim that here, Zion is presented as mother of the nations.[52] Erich Zenger, for example, argues that Psalm 87 presents a great "world family," in which Zion, who is depicted as the mother of messianic Israel (as in Psalm 2), becomes the mother of all humanity.[53]

In order to make sense of this metaphor and to understand how the city of Zion came to be personified as a woman, some background is required. In the Hebrew Bible, the city of Zion was plausibly depicted as a female figure, in part because West Semitic and Hellenistic cities were grammatically feminine and conceived in feminine terms. In addition, Sumerian and Assyrian city laments featured a lamenting goddess and a city personified as a woman. Because cities in the vicinity of Israel were imbued with feminine characteristics, either by their feminine grammatical forms or by way of association with goddesses, it makes sense that Israel would also imagine its cities, particularly its most beloved city, in feminine terms.

---

49. The hiphil form of *zkr* could be translated as "I cause to remember," but more often it is understood in the sense of "I will mention" or "I will tell of." Here it seems to have the sense of "proclaim" or "declare" as in Isa 12:4; Jer 4:16.

50. I understand the lamed as a lamed of purpose. Waltke and O'Connor, *Biblical Hebrew Syntax*, 11.2.d (see # 41–45). However, it could indicate a datival lamed ("to those who know me").

51. *Zkr* in v. 4a may govern this phrase as well.

52. Theodore Booij lists sixteen different possible reconstructions of this psalm that consists of seven verses ("Observations," 16–25).

53. Erich Zenger claims that "the 'world revolution' pictured in Psalm 2 is transformed in Psalm 87 into a great 'world family,' when Zion as the mother of messianic Israel (Psalm 2) and as the mother of all humanity (Psalm 87) becomes the 'capitol' of the king of the world, YHWH himself" (Zenger, "Zion as Mother," 160).

In terms of the range and development of the metaphor, the city of Jerusalem is personified as a daughter under threat in First Isaiah (1:7–9; 10:32; 16:1; 37:22) and in Jeremiah (4:19–21, 29–31; 6:1–8, 22–26). Hosea is the first of the prophets to personify Israel as the wayward, adulterous wife of YHWH. The image of the city of Zion as the adulterous wife of YHWH gets picked up in Isa 1:21–26 and intensified in Jeremiah (Jer 2:2–4:2; 13:20–27) and reaches a horrifying climax in Ezekiel (16; 23). The exilic book of Lamentations features a destroyed, humiliated and mourning city/woman, Daughter Zion. Zion imagery in Second Isaiah rhetorically rebuilds and reglorifies the city for exiles in Babylon but retains the feminine personification, often depicting Zion as a mother.

The complex metaphor of the city of God as "feminine" is potentially problematic. There are numerous examples in history of associations of the feminine with geographical spaces (cities, countries, and the like). Many feminists have concluded that the feminization of space suggests a male attempt to construct a safe space, clearly delineated by well-defined boundaries; such defined space is identified with the female because it is the female that can and should be dominated and domesticated. [54]

As problematic as the feminization of space has been, as Luce Irigaray has suggested, in the space/woman pair, one cannot move without the other. Feminists need to examine the two, space and woman, together in order to "pry them out of them what they have borrowed that is feminine, from the feminine, to make them 'render up' and give back what they owe the feminine."[55] Therefore, one way to challenge problematic constructions of woman (as mirror, springboard, matter, etc.) is to use the same tool that has inscribed the body of woman. "The tool is not a feminine attribute but woman may re-utilize its marks on her, in her . . . to get back inside their ever so coherent systems."[56] Therefore, in this link between space and the female body, there may lie a means to resist a dominant

---

54. Kay Schaffer's work reveals links in Australia's history between the masculine (which is identified with man, empire and civilization) and the subduing of the feminine (associated with woman, earth, and native). She concludes that *she* is identified with land while *he* is identified with the sacred (Schaffer, *Women and Bush*). Similarly, Luce Irigaray suggests that "woman" is depicted as body matter for man to imprint, "the 'matter' on which he will always return to plant his foot in order to spring farther, leap higher" (Irigaray, *Speculum*, 34).

55. Irigaray, *This Sex*, 150.

56. Ibid.

ideology.[57] The comparison of space and the female body complicates the identity of both terms.[58]

Indeed in postbiblical texts, the image of Zion as feminine from the Hebrew Bible transcends its patriarchal and political beginnings and becomes an eschatological symbol of peace. Even in the Hebrew Bible itself, images of Zion as mother offer positive ways for the church to envision its role in the world. For Christl Maier, Psalm 87 offers a unique portrayal of Zion as the spiritual mother of all humanity. Maier argues that in Psalm 87, which represents one of the latest phases of the Zion tradition's development, the "message of this postexilic Zion song leads far beyond the traditional Zion ideology" and forms a bridge between the depiction of Zion in the Hebrew Bible and the Jewish-Hellenistic adaptation of the Zion tradition, in which Jerusalem becomes a eschatological city and a universal symbol of peace and salvation.[59]

The church as a feminine procreative space, in which people from diverse backgrounds and cultures are birthed and nurtured, is a potentially enlivening and enriching metaphor. At its best, the church has traditionally embraced the role of nurturing the spiritual, emotional, and physical needs, not only of its members, but also of people beyond its doors. The metaphor of Zion as mother of the nations could lead churches to embrace a protective or nurturing role with regard to people of diverse backgrounds and religious affiliations.

## Conclusion: Multivalency in Zion

The poets and prophets of the Hebrew Bible refuse to allow the city of Zion to remain a staid and status quo construction. Metaphors of Zion are deployed in positive and negative ways to undermine royal ideologies that tried to domesticate not only Zion but also God by implying that their affiliation with Zion offered them immunity from charges of corruption and injustice. The same "tools" that the elite gathered to promote their agenda were used against them by the prophets and even the psalms. The metaphor of Zion as refuge was so live that ultimately it took on a life of its own so to speak. In the hands of the psalmists, Zion becomes a

57. Best, "Sexualizing Space," 188.

58. Such a disruption is in line with Irigaray's larger project to reject all systems of opposition on which our culture is structured (body/soul, nature/culture, man/woman).

59. Maier, *Daughter Zion*, 8, 205–10.

haven for social justice; in the hands of Jeremiah, Zion becomes a woman who refuses to stay in Jerusalem when it is overrun with crime and greed; in Lamentations, the woman Zion weeps for the loss of her people and witnesses to the harshness of God's punishment; and Second Isaiah announces the reconciliation of the estranged couple, Zion and YHWH, and the rebuilding of the precious city. Zion is daughter, whore, queen, mother, pilgrimage site, sacred city, and navel of creation. This range of the metaphors indicates that the city of Zion cannot simply be characterized as a passive and inferior space inscribed by men who viewed themselves as representing culture and the sacred.

In the Zion Songs (particularly in Ps 48), God and Zion become a unity. The boundaries between male and female, heaven and earth, god and humanity are fundamentally blurred. What enables such a breakdown in boundaries is, in part, the overlap in the metaphorical schema itself. In the Psalter, both God *and* Zion are proclaimed to be "our refuge." In Zion, where God dwells, divine presence is so palpable and compelling that God becomes indistinguishable from God's dwelling place. God is our refuge (Pss 2:12; 18:1–2; 46:1, 7, 11) *and* Zion is the geographical embodiment of that refuge. In Zion, Israel strives to live into God's call and covenant to be a people set apart from, yet deeply committed to and rooted in the world.

The biblical metaphor of Zion as refuge is one replete with multivalence and indeterminacy. The complex contours of the metaphor enable it to resist the categorization and reductionism so often associated with biblical interpretation that leads to oppression and violence. If the postmodern church can live into and be inspired by the depth, breadth, and general irreducibility of biblical metaphors and loosen its grasp on a desire for certitude, perhaps it might find itself invigorated.

# BIBLIOGRAPHY

Banana, Canaan S. "The Case for a New Bible." In *"Rewriting" the Bible: The Real Issues; Perspectives from within Biblical and Religious Studies in Zimbabwe*, edited by Isabel Mukonyora et al., 17–32. Religious and Theological Studies Series 1. Gweru, Zimbabwe: Mambo, 1993.

Best, Sue. "Sexualizing Space." In *Sexy Bodies: The Strange Carnalities of Feminism*, edited by Elizabeth Grosz and Elspeth Probyn, 181–94. London: Routledge, 1995.

Booij, Theodore. "Some Observations on Psalm LXXXVII." *Vetus Testamentum* 37 (1987) 16–25.

Brown, William P. *Seeing the Psalms: A Theology of Metaphor.* Louisville: Westminster John Knox, 2002.

Brueggemann, Walter. "Trajectories in Old Testament Literature and the Sociology of Ancient Israel." In *A Social Reading of the Old Testament: Prophetic Approaches to Israel's Communal Life,* edited by Patrick D. Miller, 13–42. Minneapolis: Fortress, 1994.

Camp, Claudia. "Metaphor in Feminist Biblical Interpretation: Theoretical Perspectives." *Semeia* 61 (1993) 3–38.

Clements, R. E. *God and Temple: The Idea of Divine Presence in Ancient Israel.* Oxford: Blackwell, 1965.

Clifford, Richard J. *The Cosmic Mountain in Canaan and the Old Testament.* Havard Semitic Monographs 4. Cambridge: Harvard University Press, 1972.

Collins, John J. *Does the Bible Justify Violence?* Facets. Minneapolis: Fortress, 2004.

———. "The Zeal of Phineas: The Bible and the Legitimation of Violence." *Journal of Biblical Literature* 122 (2003) 3–21.

Creach, Jerome F. D. *Yahweh as Refuge and the Editing of the Hebrew Psalter.* Journal for the Study of the Old Testament Supplement Series 217. Sheffield: Sheffield Academic, 1996.

Dube, Musa. "'Go Therefore and Make Disciples of All Nations' (Matt 28:19a): A Postcolonial Perspective on Biblical Criticism and Pedagogy." In *Teaching the Bible: The Discourses and Politics of Biblical Pedagogy,* edited by Fernando F. Segovia and Mary Ann Tolbert, 224–54. Maryknoll, NY: Orbis, 1998.

Elgin, Suzette Haden. "Response from the Perspective of a Linguist." *Semeia* 61 (1993) 209–17.

Eliade, Mircea. *The Myth of the Eternal Return: Or, Cosmos and History.* Translated by W. R. Trask. Bollingen Series 46. Princeton: Princeton University Press, 1971.

Hood, J. Larry. *Visions of Zion: Christianity, Modernization and the American Pursuit of Liberty Progressivism in Rural Nelson and Washington Counties, Kentucky.* Lanham, MD: University Press of America, 2005.

Irigaray, Luce. *Speculum of the Other Woman.* Translated by Gillian C. Gill. Ithaca, NY: Cornell University Press, 1985.

———. *This Sex Which Is Not One.* Translated by Catherine Porter, with Carolyn Burke. Ithaca, NY: Cornell University Press, 1985.

Kittay, Eva Feder. *Metaphor: Its Cognitive Force and Linguistic Structure.* Clarendon Library of Logic and Philosophy. Oxford: Clarendon, 1987.

Kwok, Pui-Lan. *Discovering the Bible in the Non-Biblical World.* Bible & Liberation Series. Maryknoll, NY: Orbis, 1995.

Lakoff, George, and Mark Johnson. *Metaphors We Live By.* Chicago: University of Chicago Press, 1980.

Lakoff, George, and Mark Turner. *More Than Cool Reason: A Field Guide to Poetic Metaphor.* Chicago: University of Chicago Press, 1989.

Levenson, Jon. *Sinai and Zion: An Entry into the Jewish Bible.* New Voices in Biblical Studies. Minneapolis: Winston, 1985. Reprinted, San Francisco: Harper & Row, 1987.

Lyotard, Jean-Francois. *The Postmodern Condition: A Report on Knowledge.* Translated by Geoff Bennington and Brian Massumi. Theory and History of Literature 10. Minneapolis: University of Minnesota Press, 1984.

Mac Cormac, Earl. *A Cognitive Theory of Metaphor.* Cambridge: MIT Press, 1985.

Maier, Christl M. *Daughter Zion, Mother Zion: Gender, Space, and the Sacred in Ancient Israel*. Minneapolis: Fortress, 2008.

Miller, Patrick D. "The Ruler in Zion and the Hope of the Poor: Psalms 9–10 in the Context of the Psalter." In *David and Zion: Biblical Studies in Honor of J. J. M. Roberts*, edited by Bernard F. Batto and Kathryn L. Roberts, 187–98. Winona Lake, IN: Eisenbrauns, 2004.

Ollenburger, Ben C. *Zion, the City of the Great King: A Theological Symbol of the Jerusalem Cult*. Journal for the Study of the Old Testament Supplement Series 41. Sheffield: JSOT Press, 1987.

Roberts, J. J. M. "The Davidic Origin of the Zion Tradition." In *The Bible and the Ancient Near East: Collected Essays*, 313–30. Winona Lake, IN: Eisenbrauns, 2002.

———. "The End of War in the Zion Tradition: The Imperialistic Background of an Old Testament Vision of Worldwide Peace." In *Character Ethics and the Old Testament: Moral Dimensions of Scripture*, edited by M. Daniel Carroll R., and Jacqueline E. Lapsley, 119–28. Louisville: Westminster John Knox, 2007.

———. "The Enthronement of YHWH and David: The Abiding Theological Significance of the Kingship of the Language of the Psalms." *Catholic Biblical Quarterly* 64 (2002) 675–86.

Rossing, Daniel. "Zion." In *A Dictionary of Jewish-Christian Relations*, edited by Edward Kessler and Neil Wenbon, 450–51. Cambridge: Cambridge University Press / Cambridge Centre for the Study of Jewish-Christian Relations, 2005.

Scarry, Elaine. *On Beauty and Being Just*. Princeton: Princeton University Press, 2001.

Schaffer, Kay. *Women and the Bush: Forces of Desire in the Australian Cultural Tradition*. Cambridge: Cambridge University Press, 1988.

Schroer, Silvia. "'We Will Know Each Other by Our Fruits': Feminist Exegesis and the Hermeneutics of Liberation." In *Feminist Interpretation of the Bible and the Hermeneutics of Liberation*, edited by Silvia, and Sophia Bietenhard, 1–18. Journal for the Study of the Old Testament Supplement Series 374. Sheffield: Sheffield Academic, 2003.

Sorg, Rembert. *Ecumenic Psalm 87: Original Form and Two Rereadings*, with an appendix on Psalm 119:3. Fifield, WI: King of Martyrs Priory, 1969.

Stadelmann, Andreas. "Psalm 87 (86)—Theologischer Gehalt und gesellschaftliche Wirkung." In *Ein Gott, eine Offenbarung: Beitragezur biblischen Exegese, Theologie und Spirtualitat: Festschrift fur Notker Fuglister OSB zum 60. Geburstag*, edited by Friedrich V. Reiterer, 333–56. Wurzburg: Echter, 1991.

Tsumura, David T. "The Literary Structure of Psalm 46." *Annual of the Japanese Biblical Institute* 6 (1980) 29–55.

Waltke, Bruce K., and Michael P. O'Connor. *An Introduction to Biblical Hebrew Syntax*. Winona Lake, IN: Eisenbrauns, 1990.

Weiser, Artur. *The Psalms: A Commentary*. Old Testament Library. Philadelphia: Westminster, 1962.

Williamson, Clark M. *A Guest in the House of Israel: Post-Holocaust Church Theology*. Louisville: Westminster John Knox, 1993.

Zenger, Erich. "Zion as Mother of the Nations." In *The God of Israel and the Nations: Studies in Isaiah and the Psalms*, edited by Norbert Lohfink and Erich Zenger, 123–60. Collegeville, MN: Liturgical, 2000.

# Pastoral Response

## Janet Forbes

### From Tourists to Pilgrims

A S A PASTOR, I first noticed spiritual tourists in the events surrounding tragic loss. The throngs of people who came to the church were not familiar with sacred words or the etiquette of grief. They stood outside the building in huddles of care, clinging to one another, smoking, sighing, tugging at their clothing, knowing intuitively that they had broken some kind of dress code. But they came, bringing with them a desperate hope of finding Something that would make sense of the senseless.

While I was serving in Cheyenne, Wyoming, I officiated at the funeral for the first casualty of the Iraq War, an army ranger, who died in Baghdad after his helicopter was shot down. Just five weeks after the events of September 11, the tourists who crowded into the civic auditorium were emotionally raw and spiritually outraged. The governor and members of Congress joined armed services leaders to salute this twenty-year-old husband, son, and soldier. Lee Greenwood provided the music for the occasion, *Proud to Be an American.*

Kendall, a thirteen-year-old girl who knew the young widow, tried to interpret our shared loss. She read the obituary from the local newspaper. Having never seen a death notice, she quoted, "Survivors: wife, Mary; parents, Ed and Susan; brother, Andrew; sister, Ellen; all of Cheyenne." To Kendall, every person in Cheyenne was a beneficiary of this young man's sacrifice. She made meaning out of the meaningless, knowing that her friend gave his life so that all of the citizens of Cheyenne could survive.

Kendall is a spiritual tourist, one of the many who journey to churches to understand the devastating events that happen in their lives. "They are the unmoored nomads in a fractured world trying to make spiritual and theological sense of the changes, violence, suffering, and war that have engulfed us."[1]

I thought of Kendall when the choir from my congregation went to New York City to sing in a choral festival at the Lincoln Center. On our sightseeing afternoon, we visited Ground Zero and St. Paul's Chapel, the church that sits on the edge of the site of the World Trade Center. Since September 2001, this congregation has seen more than two million visitors a year.

While watching the people interact with the displays from the days following 9/11, I spoke with the rector about spiritual tourists—the crowds of people who come to the church to understand the terrorist attacks. The clergywoman said, "We've got tourists galore. Since the reconstruction has begun, people come here to remember those days. Oh, they come. Choirs want to sing. Artists want to paint. They come by the thousands, every day. But I don't want them to leave as tourists. I want them to become pilgrims. I want them to connect, to know that there is something more."

Although few churches have two million tourists a year, St. Paul's is not necessarily unique. In effect, these words describe all religious communities. Every church, synagogue, mosque, and temple in the United States sits among a throng of tourists—people on a journey of self-discovery, or the spiritually homeless, all seeking a community of understanding. But simply being on a spiritual journey does not automatically mean that people will find meaning. Rather, as the rector suggested, they need to connect and discover that journeys can become pilgrimages. Tourists can become pilgrims. The homeless can find a place of refuge.

Spiritual homelessness arises in the failure of existing or former religious pathways to mediate religious experience, thus augmenting the sense of spiritual tourism. As I listen to the stories of those who come seeking, I discover that some have been de-churched, hurt and betrayed. "It's not safe for me to come to church. God's got it in for me and you'll all get caught in the crossfire," laughs one young adult husband whose marriage has been annulled without his consent. Others seek spiritual

---

1. Bass and Steward-Sickling, *From Nomads to Pilgrims*, xi.

growth and are skeptical about the church's relevance. "I'm gay and refuse to be labeled 'a mistake.'" Others suffer the wounds of fundamentalism. "People lied about the Bible and its claims. How can any of it be true if it is not all true?" Parents are anxious about their families. "I'm looking for some people who will love my children as much as I do. I worry that they will not survive into their twenties." Most are perpetually en route to new places, having left religious traditions and extended family to pursue education, careers, and marriages. They are living from city to suburb until the next transfer or layoff or entrepreneurial venture, trying to keep their children safe in a "Columbine world."

In her essay, Dr. Erickson has reclaimed a metaphor that affirms my commitment to forming faith communities that can listen to and honor the diversity of story that shapes individual spiritual formation. My hope is that the postmodern church will become a way-station—a refuge—for travelers who carry their diverse stories of encounter and fear into moments of intersection. When moments of intersection are interlaced with the Judeo-Christian story, the possibility exists by the power of the Spirit for community, transformation, and revelation.

In the radical hospitality of way-station ministry, the experience of refuge is life-giving. Among the spiritually homeless, I hear two pleas. The first is for spiritual direction that can bring meaning and purpose to life, a sense of inner fulfillment or satisfying devotion to something sacred. The second is healing, not simply physical and emotional healing, but wholeness and well-being that comes from facing our vicissitudes and coping with the estrangement that can overwhelm personal relationships.[2] The ministry of refuge, as affirmed in Erickson's Zion metaphor, embraces these yearnings, seeking to build a community that bears God's incarnational presence, companioning each other toward wellness and peace.

In this model, the spiritual leader becomes a fellow traveler, fellow pilgrim, fellow sufferer, or to use the Celtic term, *anamchara* (soul friend).[3] The practice of soul friending in a community of refuge is ripe with potential in the postmodern era. The soul friend concept affirms the centrality of story in a season when multiple stories define our ways of being together. By encouraging persons to individuate, that is, to articulate their own faith perspectives in safe places, and then to encourage conversation

2. Steere, *Spiritual Presence*, 13.

3. Bradley, *Colonies of Heaven*, 1.

across those differences, community might thrive in both intrafaith and interfaith settings. In a fluid, global world, leaders who attend to refuge communities will sing the songs of Zion among multifaith peoples.

As we befriend those who travel, we will reframe their stories in light of a God whose intimate presence "gathers . . . heals . . . binds up . . . [and] gives to all" (Ps 147:2–4). We will unsecularize the world and point to the holistic sacred. How good it will be to sing praises to God!

## BIBLIOGRAPHY

Bass, Diana Butler, and Joseph Steward-Sickling, editors. *From Nomads to Pilgrims: Stories from Practicing Congregations.* Herndon, VA: Alban Institute, 2006.

Bradley, Ian. *Colonies of Heaven: Celtic Models for Today's Church.* London: Darton, Longman and Todd, 2000.

Steere, David A. *Spiritual Presence in Psychotherapy: A Guide for Caregivers.* New York: Brunner/Mazel, 1997.

# Pastoral Response

## Vernon K. Rempel

### Metaphors in Church Life

"MUSIC BEGINS TO ATROPHY when it departs too far from the dance; ... poetry begins to atrophy when it gets too far from music."[1] In other words, poetry must stay close to the dance floor to retain evocative power. What is true for poetry is also true for metaphor. Words intended to be effective, moving, inspirational, or capable of conviction will be well connected to the "dance floor." To have this kind of life, the words of metaphor must spring from a place where steps are taken, where feet are on the floor, where feet are grounded. In this place, bodies move with joy and purpose. It is a place of floorboards, sweat, touch, and breath. It is not too much to say that good metaphor has a smell. At the least, it has the power of smell to transport the human imagination at light-speed into a full-textured world. Good metaphor has the power to invite us into a new world because the language has already let us "taste and see" that world.

Amy Erickson in her essay "Zion as Refuge" correctly argues for "the fundamental role of metaphor in shaping our perceptions about who we are, what we believe, and how we interact with the world around us." Such is the power of metaphors in human formation that "we do not make metaphors—rather, metaphors make us." Often the distinction is made between "talk and action," disparaging talk in favor of action, as if talk is merely like what Erickson calls "poetic embellishment" while

---

1. Pound. *The ABC of Reading*, preface.

action creates substance. I think this utterly misses the power of metaphor. Erickson is right. Good words will bring "real change in human attitudes." And attitudes translate into transformed relationships, organizations, and culture.

Where can we go for strong metaphor? Liturgical life in a faith community is a particularly rich locus for creating and appropriating metaphor that matters. Faith communities read ancient texts for contemporary meaning. We sing and pray with linguistic tropes full of metaphor for that invisible but palpable Holy Spirit, for the love that can spring to life so powerfully in human community, for the enduring hope embedded in the mysteries of life. Liturgical life is fertile seedbed for words about that which matters close to the heart and soul.

International conflict mediator Marc Gopin remarks about my own Mennonite denomination's strong practice of conflict mediation that "this method of engagement of radical humility is not just an ethical act or a strategy . . . for Mennonites. It appears to be part of their being, a cultural characteristic that is at the heart of their religious experience of divine closeness and emulation . . . The community prayers, songs, and sermons often revolve around this theme."[2] Liturgical life translates directly into ethical practice. Prayers, songs, and sermons matter; metaphors within these movements of worship are transformative.

## The Metaphor of Zion

Erickson goes on to argue for the value of biblical metaphor over against contemporary cultural metaphors. Likewise, Walter Brueggemann over and over again offers the distinction between "thick" biblical texts full of communal wisdom and divine challenge and "thin" texts of culture arising from various easy distortions, habits, and addictions.[3]

I always marvel that folks come to church. In my postmodern urban Mennonite congregation, few people come with the week-to-week religiosity of past eras. But now people come more than ever by choice, without layers of guilt or social obligation. And still they come! What is the longing met, the connection answered that brings people to church when they so easily could do something else? I think it is the relationships. But

2. Gopin, *Between Eden and Armageddon*, 153.
3. One example: Brueggemann, *Inscribing the Text*.

these are a particular kind of relationships: not the relationships of club or even workplace, but relationships centered and grounded in ancient and profound metaphor.

Erickson sounds this note. She writes: "The theological claim of divine presence in Zion is a powerful one."[4] Divine presence in Zion; God in the city. Mennonites as a faith-culture movement are only two or three generations "off the farm." For centuries, we were a pacifist rural people, offering creative and energetic farming—food production—as an alternative to joining in any nation's call to go to war. Now we have come from these "sacred villages" into the "urban village."[5] Therefore, Mennonites very much need metaphors that make sense of urban life as a place of the divine. We need to name how God is present not only in the past life of rural farming but in the "big world" of city life.

In my urban congregation, people are engaged in varied, demanding structures of the professions, of business and corporation, as public employees in school and agency. These structures can tend to arrogate themselves to a place of central and ultimate importance. Mennonite author Phyllis Pellman Good notes that the professions want to be gods in our lives.[6] The metaphor of divine presence in Zion offers the chance to let Divine Spirit decenter the idolatrous power of urban structures that are good enough but not ultimately good or capable of fundamental provision of meaning, purpose, and transformation.

## A Feminine Metaphor

What about a *feminine* metaphor for such a faith community? Erickson well says that constructing usable metaphors from the Hebrew Bible requires "navigating the patriarchal and imperial landmines." And regarding treating the city of Zion as feminine metaphor: "such defined space is identified with the female because it is the female that can and should be dominated and domesticated." My experience in biblically grounded congregational liturgy is that bringing in, celebrating, or unleashing the feminine voice is a fraught, ongoing project that requires constant vigilance and assertiveness. The cultures out of which the biblical writings

---

4. See p. 154 above.

5. Driedger, *Mennonites in the Global Village*, 7.

6. Kraybill and Good, *Perils of Professionalism*, 8.

emerge are male-dominant. Our culture continues to be male-dominant, not the least in congregational liturgy. The successful deploying of a genuinely powerful feminine metaphor would be a gift indeed. It is ever so tricky to speak out of such basic theological understandings as "God as initiator" or "prevenient grace" in a cultural situation where men are constantly, and as a default, located as actors and agents while women must always struggle against the undertow of definition as the second sex, the responding sex, the answering sex.

The metaphor of Zion as woman, as refuge, as feminine city of protection and power has the potential to help locate women in full agency, full leadership, and centered as meaning makers, history shapers, avatars of God's good future. Erickson writes: "Zion is daughter, whore, queen, mother, pilgrimage site, sacred city, and navel of creation. This range of the metaphors indicates that the city of Zion cannot simply be characterized as a passive and inferior space inscribed by men who viewed themselves as representing culture and the sacred." Now, "whore" may be a bit much on a congregational Sunday morning (but maybe not for the adult-education hour!). But the implication that woman-form or woman's body-self may intersect metaphorically with "divine city," full of echoes of generativity, protection, abundance, inclusion, and universality is wonderful hope and resource for the weekly liturgy.

One final note of practice: it matters very much who is offering this metaphor. In order for such a metaphor to do its evocative work, women must occupy liturgical and ecclesial space in the same way that a feminine Zion occupies physical and historical space. This metaphor needs to be presented in song, preaching, and prayer, but presented by women: women in the space of the pulpit, on the stage, in the roles of dialogue facilitators, community organizers, and administrators. This metaphor will best be articulated and framed by people experiencing women-in-their-bodies speaking it, and therefore offering an incarnation. Or, to paraphrase Romans 12, women may "present your bodies as a living manifestation...". Then there may be new rejoicing in the presence of "the gates of daughter Zion" (Ps 9:14 NRSV).

## BIBLIOGRAPHY

Brueggemann, Walter. *Inscribing the Text: Sermons and Prayers of Walter Brueggemann.* Edited by Anna Carter Florence. Minneapolis: Fortress, 2004.

Driedger, Leo. *Mennonites in the Global Village.* Toronto: University of Toronto Press, 2000.

Gopin, Marc. *Between Eden and Armageddon: The Future of World Religions, Violence, and Peacemaking.* Oxford: Oxford University Press, 2002.

Kraybill, Donald B., and Phyllis Pellman Good, editors. *The Perils of Professionalism: Essays on Christian Faith and Professionalism.* Scottdale, PA: Herald, 1982.

Pound, Ezra. *The ABC of Reading.* A New Directions Paperbook 89. New York: Laughlin, 1960.

# Scripture Index

# Subject Index

Stanovsky, Elaine, x, xviii, xxv, 22–25
Steere, David , 172–73
Steward-Sickling, Joseph, 171, 173
Strawbridge, Elizabeth, 54
Stuart, Elizabeth, 96, 107
Stuhr, Wally, 109
suffering, 34, 128, 131, 133, 140

Thistlethwaite, Susan Brooks, 27, 31, 44
Tillich, Paul, 160
Tinker, Tink, xi–xiii, xvii
Tisdale, Leonora T., 71, 88
tourists, spiritual, 170–71
Tracy, David, 84, 88
transformation, 24–25, 155
Trinity, 90–91
Tsumura, David, 155, 169
Tucker, Mary Orne, 12
Turner, Mark, 149
Turpin, Katherine, ix, xviii, xxvii,
    93–111
Twelve-step groups, 15

Unitarian Universalism, 124–25
Unitarian Universalist Association, 95
United Church of Christ, 95, 108
United Methodism, 4, 9, 14–20, 113
United Methodist Church, xx, xxv, 22,
    26, 71–72, 88, 93–94, 102, 107,
    108–11, 124
urbanization, 4–5, 14

Wallace, Charles, Jr., 11, 21
Waltke, Bruce, 164, 169
Washbourne, Penelope, 132, 141
Way, Peggy, 130, 142
Webb-Mitchell, Brett, 33–34, 44
Weber, Max, 18, 21
Weems, Lovett H., Jr., xix, xxx
Weiser, Artur, 163, 169
Wesley, John, xxvi, 7–10, 16–18, 21,
    51–62, 75, 99–100
Wesley, Susanna, 10–11, 13
Wigger, John, 54, 62
Wiggins, Marsha, 139, 142
Willard, Frances, 6, 14, 21, 23, 25, 100–
    102, 106–7
Williams, Carmen Braun, 139, 142
Williamson, Clark, 157, 169
wives of ministers, 12–13, 19
women
    of color, 128
    preachers, 75
Women's Christian Temperance Union,
    6, 23, 100
Wright, Dana, xxii, xxx

Zenger, Erich, 164, 169
Zion as refuge, xxviii, xxvix, xxix,
    149–70
Zion songs, 149, 158–62, 167

Made in the USA
San Bernardino, CA
16 January 2018